DATE DUE			

the dissolving image

the dissolving image

the spiritual-esthetic development
of W. B. Yeats

by Bernard Levine
Wayne State University

Wayne State University Press   Detroit 1970

Published simultaneously in Canada
by The Copp Clark Publishing Company
517 Wellington Street, West
Toronto 2B, Canada.

Library of Congress Catalog Card Number: 70-86953
Standard Book Number: 8143-1414-7

The author acknowledges permissions to quote from the following:
  "Lake Isle of Innisfree," "Lamentation of the Old Pensioner" (original and final versions), "He Reproves the Curlew," "He Hears the Cry of the Sedge," "Words," "The Dawn," "Paudeen," and "Leda and the Swan," reprinted with the permission of Mr. M. B. Yeats and Macmillan & Co. of London.
  Excerpts from *Yeats' Letters,* ed. Allan Wade. Reprinted with the permission of Miss Anne B. Yeats and Rupert Hart-Davis, Publisher.
  Excerpts from William Butler Yeats, *Essays and Introductions.* Reprinted with permission of The Macmillan Company. Copyright Mrs. W. B. Yeats, 1959.
  Excerpts from William Butler Yeats, *Mythologies.* Reprinted with the permission of The Macmillan Company. Copyright 1937 by The Macmillan Company, renewed 1965 by Bertha Georgie Yeats and Anne Butler Yeats.
  Excerpts from William Butler Yeats, *Autobiography.* Reprinted with permission of The Macmillan Company. Copyright 1916, 1936 by The Macmillan Company, renewed 1944 by Bertha Georgie Yeats.
  Excerpts from *The Variorum Edition of the Poems of W. B. Yeats,* ed. Peter Allt & Russell K. Alspach. Reprinted with the permission of The Macmillan Company. Copyright 1903, 1906, 1907, 1912, 1916, 1918, 1919, 1924, 1928, 1931, 1933, 1934, 1935, 1940, 1944, 1946, 1950, 1956, 1957, by The Macmillan Company, renewed 1968 by Bertha Georgie Yeats, Michael Butler Yeats, and Anne Butler Yeats.

dedicated in memory of
Lawrence S. Blate

. . . trying so hard
To hold our centers still
As if this little measure
Of odds and ends
Could ever matter much
In the single day
Of a blind god's life.

contents

preface

Yeats had his eye half-fixed upon the nonmaterial world, and so regarded the phenomena of life as reality in the making. He was impatient with illusions of stability, be it in regard to love, government, religion, or art; his temperament would not allow for final expression in poetry of contentment or resolution. And he came to rejoice in the art of conflict, not because he loved war or anarchy but because he felt that art could bring the expression of conflict under control. Art for Yeats was a spiritual discipline, a medium for the process of self-liberation.

The present study examines Yeats's poems as manifestations of their narrator's evolving state of mind. For Yeats, as for virtually any romantic poet—Blake, Shelley, Wordsworth, Coleridge, Keats, Hölderlin, Mallarmé, Rilke, Crane, Thomas—whose concentration of expression reflects a world other than that of the self, thereby changing the face of reality, the body of poetry must wear the mystery of a mask. The language of such poetry is most characteristic in its defiance of fixed values. Words and images assume the facade of meaning in relation to the changing symbols of some ultimate reality.

The explication of poetry is here regarded as an exploratory, not a defining process. This study, rather than postulating meaning, undertakes to test the elasticity of Yeats's language; its object is to offer an evolving perspective of the modal, imagistic, and thematic tensions in his work. Principal focus in the explication is on the imaginative action of the speaker, rather than on the concrete phenomena to which images seem to refer. The poetry mirrors in its tension the spiritual scene, from the center of which seems to emerge always more vividly the voice of the speaker: the auditory imagination at work, as T. S. Eliot would say. Yeats's poetry as a whole, then, may be viewed as external form dissolving toward its invisible center, the spiritual demesne of the speaker's self-transforming awareness.

The present volume grew out of work undertaken at Brown University under the direction of Professors Gregory Polletta and Mark Spilka, whose suggestions and criticism led to the rethinking and substantial rewriting of the manuscript. The book could not have been completed without a faculty research grant from Wayne State University. The first chapter and a portion of the last chapter were published in somewhat different form in *Universitas, 4*: 138–48, 1966 and *James Joyce Quarterly, 3*: 124–29, Winter, 1966. The study of "Leda and the Swan," part of Chapter 6, was published in *The Bucknell Review, 17*: 85–111, March, 1969.

A special debt is owing to my wife, Deborah Brown Levine, with whose encouragement and advice the seven chapters found their way through the necessary revisions.

B. L.

abbreviations

The notes, located at the back of the book, are reserved for comments on the main text and for references to secondary sources. Citations for Yeats's own works are included parenthetically in abbreviated form throughout the book. The following is an explanation of the abbreviations thus used:

A   *The Autobiography of William Butler Yeats, Consisting of Reveries over Childhood and Youth, the Trembling of the Veil and Dramatis Personae,* Garden City, 1958.

E   *Essays and Introductions.* London, 1961.

EX   *Explorations,* selected by Mrs. W. B. Yeats. New York, 1963.

IF   *If I were Four-and-Twenty.* Dublin, 1940.

KT   *Letters to Katharine Tynan,* ed. Roger McHugh. New York, 1953.

L   *The Letters of W. B. Yeats,* ed. Alan Wade. London, 1954.

LP   *Letters on Poetry from W. B. Yeats to Dorothy Wellesley.* London, 1940.

M   *Mythologies.* New York, 1959.

OB   *On the Boiler.* Dublin, 1939.

P   *The Variorum Edition of the Poems of W. B. Yeats,* ed. Peter Allt and Russell Alspach. New York, 1957.

PC   *Plays and Controversies.* London, 1923.

PL   *The Collected Plays of W. B. Yeats.* New York, 1953.

V   *A Vision.* (A reissue with the author's final revisions.) New York, 1961.

WB   *Wheels and Butterflies.* London, 1934.

YM   *W. B. Yeats and T. Sturge Moore: Their Correspondence,* ed. Ursula Bridge. New York, 1953.

chapter 1

Yeats's esthetics and his concept of the self

In his prose writings Yeats gives ample evidence that his concern with esthetics has an underlying spiritual basis. In the only book-length study of Yeats's esthetics, *The Vast Design* (1964), Edward Engelberg has dealt with the symbolic intension of the poet's imaginative process, relating his methods of thinking and composition to what Coleridge called the "secondary imagination": the assumption that images and ideas should concentrate in their expression a "multeity" of associations. In this present study I would like to shift the focus of attention from the image to the Self[1]—the transpersonalizing (though not impersonal[2]) voice behind the flow of images—and from this vantage point investigate Yeats's aptitude for what, in his play *The Resurrection,* he calls "spiritual reality."

Yeats counted on the use of a persona, or mask, to communicate the sense of spiritual reality. The self-centered concerns of life made for only limited awareness. By adopting one of several psychodramatic roles for his expression of passion (Richard Ellmann calls it "affirmative capability") he would be able to separate from his lesser self sufficiently to project an archetypal awareness:

> The creative power of the lyric poet depends upon his accepting some one of a few traditional attitudes, lover, sage, hero, scorner of life. They bring us back to the spiritual norm. They may, however, . . . so act upon the events of our lives as to compel us to attend to that perfection which, though it seems theirs, is the work of our own *Daimon.* (*V,* 234)

For Yeats passionate detachment allows for the expression of an energy characteristic not of oneself, one's own private emotions, but of related transpersonal "norms." The exercise of such energy is at once the cause and the result of Yeats's enlarged comprehension of the Self, identified in this passage from *A Vision* as his spiritual Daimon.[3]

The relationship between the poet and his art is intense, but the poet and the art are separate, each working on the other, much the same as in a mask relationship. *"When ever I remake a song,"* Yeats wrote, *". . . / It is myself that I remake"* (*P*, 778). The poem is made to reflect the perfection that the poet wants to achieve, and so helps collapse the poet's ego (*E*, 522). Similarly, for an audience the conflict of pure passion can finally diminish awareness of the individual self:

> If the subject of drama or any other art, were a man himself, an eddy of momentary breath, we might desire the contemplation of perfect characters; but the subject of all art is passion, and a passion can only be contemplated when separated by itself, purified of all but itself, and aroused into a perfect intensity by opposition with some other passion. . . . (*PC*, 105)

"The human soul," Yeats declared, "would not be conscious were it not suspended between contraries." (*P*, 824).

Only by a separation from the terrestrial condition, from society, from "everything that is not itself," Yeats maintained, can the arts simulate the ambience of a "spiritual reality."

> The arts are at their greatest when they seek for a life growing always more scornful of everything that is not itself and passing into its own fullness, as it were, ever more completely as all that is created out of the passing mode of society slips from it. (*PC*, 123)

Social "curiosities" had found their place in Victorian poetry, and such "curiosities," Yeats felt, art had to get free of:

> I saw . . . that Swinburne in one way, Browning in another, and Tennyson in a third, had filled their work with what I called "impurities," curiosities about politics, about science, about history, about religion; and that we must create once more the pure work. (*A*, 112)

The artist, Yeats was convinced, must enter into a dialogue with art in order to purify his mind of "curiosities" and "heterogeneous knowledge." Only in this way can he come into an awareness of something larger than himself—and more momentous than the circumstantial life around him:

> The more a poet rids his verse of heterogeneous knowledge and irrelevant analysis, and purifies his mind with elaborate art, the more does

Self intrudes on passion so must use masks & persona or explore the spiritual passionate world the little ritual of his verse resemble the great ritual of Nature, and become mysterious and inscrutable. He becomes, as all the great mystics have believed, a vessel of the creative power of God. (*E,* 201–202)

The artist in time realizes that what he intuits as "the creative power of God" is really the power of his own Daimon, and that "a God is but the Self" (*E,* 461).

Yeats did not subscribe to the "pure art" as practiced by Mallarmé and Valéry, but he did want an art that was purified of everything that did not lead to a realization of Self and to an awareness of "spiritual reality." Yeats thought of creative power and artistic discipline as a means of discovering the energy of "pure life." And although artistic creation followed hours of thoughtful labor, it was not a "deliberate creation" but the spontaneous flow of "intense feeling" (*PC,* 102).

Art, then, for Yeats has a separate but not an independent existence. The poem is the verbalized manifestation of pure energy which the poet identifies with what is "permanent" in the world (*PC,* 102). Form evolves from an imaginative ordering of pure energy and is the kind of permanence which renders the work of art beautiful. A work of art that is beautiful can be experienced over and again and each time will crystallize in the mind something that had not before been realized. The more profound the mystery or "secret knowledge" that goes into the creative process, Yeats believed, the more beautiful will be the form which the finished product assumes. And so the depth and permanence of a work of art we may regard as relative to the symbolizing intensity of the mind.

What continues to surprise, shock, or give pleasure is for Yeats a basis for poetry, the medium through which the symbolic imagination attempts to discover the mind's, or the soul's, regenerating force. The creative act thus reveals what is organic and cyclic, rather than what is fixed, within "the soul of the world." And the glorification of such art, therefore, consists in the passionate awareness of what is least permanent in the material world. This view is best set forth in *Discoveries:*

If it be true that God is a circle whose centre is everywhere, the saint goes to the centre, the poet and artist to the ring where everything comes round again. The poet must not seek for what is still and fixed, for that has no life for him; and if he did his style would become cold and monotonous, and his sense of beauty faint and sickly, . . . but be content to find his pleasure in all that is for ever passing away that it may come again, in the beauty of woman, in the fragile flowers of spring, in momentary heroic passion, in whatever is most fleeting, most impassioned, as it were, for its own perfection, most eager to return in its glory. (*E*, 287–88)

The "passions" give to art its organic form and beauty. Yeats differentiates the passion of the poet from the counterpassion of the "saint." The "saint" has surrendered up his creative energy for the sake of an external ideal:

> No mind is more valuable than the image it contains. The imaginative writer differs from the saint in that he identifies himself—to the neglect of his own soul, alas!—with the soul of the world, and frees himself from all that is impermanent in that soul, an ascetic not of women and wine, but of the newspapers.[4] Those things that are permanent in the soul of the world, the great passions that trouble all and have but a brief recurring life of flower and seed in any man, are indeed renounced by the saint, who seeks not an eternal art, but his own eternity. The artist stands between the saint and the world of impermanent things, and just in so far as his mind dwells on what is impermanent in his sense, on all that 'modern experience and the discussion of our interests,' that is to say, on what never recurs, as desire and hope, terror and weariness, spring and autumn [manifestations of the "great passions"] recur, will his mind losing rhythm grow critical, as distinguished from creative, and his emotions wither. (*E*, 286)

For Yeats, as for Blake, "what is permanent and recurring" can be discovered only if the old forms and structures are broken down. And like Wordsworth, Yeats, in this connection, was necessarily concerned with the effective correlation of sound and feeling: he believed that each innovation in poetry depended upon dissolving the distinction between metrical movement in poetry and the imaginative "impulse" which gives birth to expression. The result would be a more refined imitation of spiritual reality.

> Every generation has more and more loosened the rhythm, more and more broken up and disorganized, for the sake of subtlety of detail, those great rhythms which move, as it were, in masses of sound. Poetry has become more spiritual, for the soul is of all things the most delicately organised. (*E*, 380)

How the soul is organized (a Blakean notion) can be discovered not in the reflection of external form, or physical movement, but in the reflective intensity of the mind's eye.

> We should come to understand that the beryl stone was enchanted by
> our fathers that it might enfold the pictures in its heart, and not to
> mirror our own excited faces, or the boughs waving outside the window.
> With this change of substance, this return to imagination, this under-
> standing that the laws of art, which are the hidden laws of the world,
> can alone bind the imagination, would come a change of style and we
> would cast out of serious poetry those energetic rhythms, as of a man
> running, which are the invention of the will with its eyes always on some-
> thing to be done or undone; and we would seek out those wavering,
> meditative, organic rhythms, which are the embodiment of the imagina-
> tion. (*E, 163*)

"Rhythms which are the embodiment of the imagination" can be
conveyed best by the speaking voice, the subtle intonations, and the feelings that the voice communicates. In reading his essay "Modern Poetry"
Yeats told his radio audience: "When I have read you a poem I have
tried to read it rhythmically; . . . there is no other method. A poem is
an elaboration of the rhythms of common speech and their associations
with profound feeling" (*E, 508*).

Yeats, like Wordsworth, was interested in absorbing "common
speech" and the "common idiom" (*L, 462*) into the rhythms of the poetic imagination. This had become a concern of his since his trips into
the back country of Sligo and Galway with his uncle George Pollexfen
and his close friend Lady Gregory, and it was a concern which became
primary once he had taken up writing for the theater. For poetry to become "common speech" an audience had to be made to concentrate
upon the organizing pattern and the spoken word, not the external
show, of a dramatic presentation; by this means the distance between
actor and audience would gradually be erased.

> Modern acting and recitation have taught us to fix our attention on the
> gross effects till we have come to think gesture, and the intonation that
> copies the accidental surface of life, more important than the rhythm. . . .
> I am certain that, if people would listen for a while to lyrical verse spoken
> to notes [the range of notes which could be obtained on the psaltery],
> they would soon find it impossible to listen without indignation to verse
> as it is spoken in our leading theatres. They would get a subtlety of
> hearing that would demand new effects from actors and even from
> public speakers, and they might, it may be, begin even to notice one
> another's voices till poetry and rhythm had come nearer to common life.
> (*E, 18–19*)

Yeats cultivated an art that was aural rather than visual, and like earlier
symbolists he made language serve as a ground for the imagination. The

effect conveyed by images of sound would be hypnotic, "monotonous," bringing the sympathetic audience to a subtler level of comprehension of relationships. And the felt resonance and rhythm of words would become so refined as to surprise with "a variety as incalculable as the outline of faces." After having experimented with the psaltery, as a means of training his ear to less familiar intervals of sound than can be obtained by using a diatonic scale—"we reject all professional singers because no mouth trained to the modern scale can articulate poetry" [5]—Yeats concluded that:

> All art is, indeed, a monotony in external things for the sake of an interior variety, a sacrifice of gross effects to subtle effects, an asceticism of the imagination. But this new art, new in modern life, I mean, will have to train its hearers as well as its speakers, for it takes time to surrender gladly the gross effects one is accustomed to, and one may well find mere monotony at first where one soon learns to find a variety as incalculable as in the outline of faces or in the expression of eyes. (*E*, 18)

The magnetic effect in art conveyed by a monotony of rhythm thus succeeds in sounding out the delicate organization of the soul, the source for Yeats of the symbolic or spiritual imagination. "If the real world is not altogether rejected, it is but touched here and there, and into the places we have left empty we summon rhythm, balance, pattern, images that remind us of vast passions, the vagueness of past times, all the chimeras that haunt the edge of trance" (*E*, 243).

In tapping the energy of the imagination the mind slips into a half-conscious, meditative state, "between sleeping and waking," getting loose, as it were, of the habitual associations which link it to the world outside. Rhythm and pattern serve to sink the mind in on itself, the trance-like quality of the verse serving finally to refine the senses: to awaken the mind to a more subtle, more illuminating sense of reality (*E*, 159). The sort of meditative trance which makes for poetic expression closes out the world and allows the mind to contemplate its own experience, drawing more deeply into the unconscious, so that eventually the poet senses an underlying, formative, or archetypal energy creating patterns and images which are suggestive of "vast passions."

For Yeats, then, art is conceived as an internalized force, and results from an intensity that approaches "stillness" and "silence." [6] The rhythm which stirs the imagination seems to blend physical and mental energy, enabling thereby a certain "passionate" self-control. Through his study of the structure of the Japanese Noh play, Yeats was able to realize in his own art form this internalizing process. In the Noh, Yeats observed,

> There are few swaying movements of arms or body such as make the beauty of our dancing. They [the dancers] move from the hip, keeping constantly the upper part of their body still, and seem to associate with every gesture or pose some definite thought. (*E*, 231)

The spiritual synthesis of natural forces represents the "ideal of beauty" in Eastern art. In the Japanese Noh the containment of physical energy approached the ideal Yeats came to feel was inherent in his own aims as poet and dramatist: to make his most passionate art reflect a "marmorean stillness." [7]

If it is true, as Dorothy Wellesley reports (*LP*, 189), that Yeats felt he "never had any physical energy," it is perhaps because he exhausted it through spiritual intensity. Yeats turned from the external world and from private emotion (both of which he refers to as mere "life") in response to his sense of mystery. Thus he speaks of love as a "passion" we experience by "choosing that beauty which seems unearthly . . . as though life were trembling into stillness and silence." (*E*, 243–44). For Yeats, the symbolic imagination draws into itself "the whole of life," and by this means the poet transmutes the idealizing energy of the mind into realization of an inner form.

For Yeats the strength of the imagination depends upon dissolution of the notion of an external idea and upon the transformation of outward-directed energy. The mental concentration induced with "the intensity of trance" allows for the deepening revelation of the unconscious, and for the consequent emergence of archetypal images. The function of art, Yeats believed, is to focus attention upon the imagination, and this can be done by an expressivistic energy analogous to the unconscious energy which accompanies the trance state. An expressivistic energy results from the articulation of "passion"—the transpersonal or "pure" emotion characterizing spiritual freedom (manifested, for example, as "tragic joy"). "Tragic art" (such as *King Lear* and *Hamlet*, or *The King's Threshold* and *The Unicorn from the Stars*) dramatizes the movement of the imagination toward an internalized state of being:

> Tragic art, passionate art, the drowner of dykes, the confounder of understanding, moves us by setting us to reverie, by alluring us almost to the

> intensity of trance. The persons upon the stage, let us say, greaten till
> they are humanity itself. We feel our minds expand convulsively or
> spread out slowly like some moon-brightened image-crowded sea. That
> which is before our eyes perpetually vanishes and returns again in the
> midst of the excitement it creates, and the more enthralling it is, the
> more do we forget it. (*E*, 245)

Because the expression of "passion" fastens our minds upon the energy
of imagination, we, as an audience, are able actually to perceive the un-
folding of the archetypal proportions of "persons upon the stage." At the
same time, the mind opens out, blossoms, as it were, to its own range of
images. Our imagination, therefore, alternately pulsates to the images of
our own experience and to the images of the art-form which commands
and concentrates our attention: by this process, the drama or the art, as
it "vanishes and returns again," stimulates and intensifies the imagination—and the imagination tends to consume the images which have
thereby served their purpose. Such art results in a steadily increasing
"excitement" or "passion," the very intensity of which finally relieves the
need for self-expression.

Yeats uses the image of "fire" to describe the condition of the self
after the self moves beyond the object-oriented—private, personal, or terrestrial—reality; the image of "fire" as used to describe an inherent reality seems to have taken hold in Yeats's mind from its metaphorical association with the creative process—referring, that is, both to the energy
which underlies the process of imagination and to the excitement which
accompanies the expression, or release, of "passion." Consider in this respect the following passage from *Discoveries:*

> There is something of an old wives' tale in fine literature. . . . He [the
> "maker" of literature] has felt something in the depth of his mind and
> he wants to make it as visible and powerful to our senses as possible.
> He will use the most extravagant words or illustrations if they suit his
> purpose. Or he will invent a wild parable, and the more his mind is on
> fire or the more creative it is, the less will he look at the outer world or
> value it for its own sake. It gives him metaphors and examples, and that
> is all. He is even a little scornful of it, for it seems to him while the fit
> is on that the fire has gone out of it and left but white ashes [cf. Shelley's
> notion of the imagination as a "fading coal"]. I cannot explain it, but I am
> certain that every high thing was invented in this way. (*E*, 276–77)

That there may be a fertile area in the mind for creative activity, the
"fire" must have been transplanted from the outer to the inner reality.

For an audience the analogous transition will have been prepared for by the poet's having made the reference to things in "the outer world" metaphorical: objective nature and the external reality to which images refer will thus become simply "a signature" of spiritual reality.

For Yeats "fire" or "conflagration" represents that energy of the imagination which gradually transforms the mind. In seeking a higher reality the imagination consumes the "temporal" image, and insofar as images originate in the imagination they indicate the quality of the mind, in terms of its lucidity and degree of refinement. "Fire" (culminating the classical elements of the Greek philosophers—earth, water, air) is for Yeats the purifying element identical with the aspiration of the self. The creative imagination which embodies this aspiration discovers, or even becomes, through the probing use of images, the phoenix "born out of the fire." Images thus fuse into symbol, the energy of the mind concentrated at its most intense moment—a vibrant and lucid form that has emerged from *Anima Mundi*.

> The minds that swayed these seemingly fluid images had doubtless form, and those images themselves seemed, as it were, mirrored in a living substance whose form is but change of form [*Anima Mundi*]. From tradition and perception, one thought of one's own life as symbolised by earth, the place of heterogeneous things, the images as mirrored in water, and the images themselves one could divine but as air; and beyond it all there were, I felt confident, certain aims and governing loves, the fire that makes all simple. Yet the images themselves were fourfold, and one judged their meaning in part from the predominance of one out of the four elements, or that of the fifth element, the veil hiding another four, a bird born out of the fire. (*M*, 46–47)

The imagination is executor and witness to the transformation from the terrestrial world to the "condition of fire." Imaginative energy elicits symbols from the unconscious, or else alchemizes into symbols images from the external world of nature. Subsequently the mind moves toward an understanding of the symbols which the imagination creates. By entering into, as it were, and attempting to unravel the symbol, the mind gradually is able to refine and purify itself (*E*, 150–51).

Yeats, like Blake, insisted that those who distrust the imagination could not achieve Self-realization. Such persons seek a spiritual being beyond the strength of their own minds, and consequently submit to a system of laws external to their nature. The symbols these persons live by become fixed and are not unravelled by the mind; they thereafter take on a reality independent of the spiritual, or creative, energy which brought them into being. This displacement of the spiritual sphere Yeats attributes to common diffidence—the conscious depreciation of Self.

> I now know that there are men who cannot possess "Unity of Being," who must not seek it or express it—and who, so far from seeking an anti-self [potentially the Self or spiritual Daimon], a Mask that delineates a being in all things the opposite to their natural state, can but seek the suppression of the anti-self, till the natural state alone remains. These are those who must seek no image of desire, but await that which lies beyond their mind—unities not of the mind, but unities of nature, unities of God . . . to hollow their hearts till they are void and without form, to summon a creator by revealing chaos, to become the lamp for another's wick and oil; and indeed it may be that it has been for their guidance in a very special sense that the "perfectly proportioned human body" suffered crucifixion. (*A*, 166–67)

The symbol is conceived to have an independent existence only if the personal self is made to reflect the limitations of nature and the mind made to postulate a perfect existence entirely apart from self and nature. This fractioning of the relationship between God, man, and nature can result only in the insubstantiality of all three. Because men choose to live in "the natural state" they flee from themselves and externalize the spiritual world; and because of "their cruelties of self-abasement" the image, or symbol, of spiritual reality becomes an oppressive rather than a Self-revealing vehicle (*A*, 167). To relocate the sense of a divine calling Yeats, like Blake, insisted on the primacy of the symbolic imagination, "the imagination which deals with spiritual things symbolized by natural things" (*L*, 343). The transition from the natural or terrestrial world to the "condition of fire" is thus effected by establishing an imaginative control over nature. Yeats expressed this idea in the well-known lines from "Sailing to Byzantium":

> O sages standing in God's holy fire
> As in the gold mosaic of a wall,
> Come from the holy fire, perne in a gyre,
> And be the singing-masters of my soul.
>
> . . . .
>
> Once out of nature I shall never take
> My bodily form from any natural thing,
> But such a form as Grecian goldsmiths make
> Of hammered gold and gold enamelling. (*P*, 408)

The "form" for which the narrator in the poem would exchange "My bodily form" is the Self, the perfect body in its "supernatural environment."

A symbol, as Yeats defines it, is a plastic image "free enough from all bonds to speak of perfection." It is the articulated form of imaginative energy constituting a "liberation" from the temporal world.

> If you liberate a person or a landscape from the bonds of motives and their actions, causes and their effects . . . it will change under your eyes, and become a symbol of an infinite emotion, a part of the Divine Essence; for we love nothing but the perfect, and our dreams make all things perfect, that we may love them. Religious and visionary people, monks and nuns, and medicine-men and opium-eaters, see symbols in their trances; for religious and visionary thought is thought about perfection and the way to perfection; and symbols are the only things free enough from all bonds to speak of perfection. (*E,* 148–49)

Yeats conceived of the imagination as fleshing out the essence of natural forms, making from "things" symbols free from the accidents of nature. In Coleridgian fashion, Yeats takes images from the external world and extracts from them their essential quality. The images thereupon become symbols of selfless energy, the "great passions": what Yeats refers to above as "infinite emotion." The excitement, or passion, which accompanies creative insight enlarges the image into symbol. The symbol reveals a stillness which contains that passion (see *V,* 185–215). Yeats further suggests that the passionate energy which typifies the imagination originates in "love." He describes "love," in the essay "Anima Mundi," as that purposive energy which presupposes a spiritual ontology, "the fire that makes all simple" (*M,* 346). "Love" is best regarded from Yeats's point of view as the intuitive force which, when crystallized as symbol, radiates from itself "the way to perfection." Its perfection, therefore, is an entirely selfless, daimonic awareness.

Only when the mind "liberated from the pressure of the will is unfolded in symbols" (*E,* 159) can there by any realization of the unconscious power of the imagination; and reflected in the perfected symbol, Yeats suggests, is one's glimpse of the Self:

> Every visionary knows that the mind's eye soon comes to see a capricious and variable world, which the will cannot shape or change, though it can call it up and banish it again. I closed my eyes a moment ago, and a company of people in blue robes swept by me in a blinding light, and

had gone before I had done more than see little roses embroidered on the hems of their robes, and confused, blossoming apple-boughs somewhere beyond them, and recognized one of the company by his square, black, curling beard. . . . I have often seen him; and one night a year ago I asked him questions which he answered by showing me flowers and precious stones, of whose meaning I had no knowledge, and he seemed too perfected a soul for any knowledge that cannot be spoken in symbol or metaphor.

Are he and his blue-robed companions, and their like, 'the eternal realities' of which we are the reflection 'in the vegetable glass of Nature,' or a momentary dream? (*E*, 151–52)

Two decades after this passage was written Yeats might have called the blue-robed figure his spiritual Daimon.

The perfection to which the daimonic vision aspires is associated by Yeats with the "invisible" or imaginative "essence" which informs the symbol. "A symbol is indeed the only possible expression of some invisible essence, a transparent lamp about a spiritual flame" (*E*, 116). The "eternal reality" which the symbol embodies thus reflects the highest, most subtle, and ultimately destructive reach of the creative imagination. "True art," Yeats writes, "is the flame of the Last Day, which begins for every man when he is first moved by beauty, and which seeks to burn all things until they become 'infinite and holy'" (*E*, 140).

True art is expressive and symbolic, and makes every form, every sound, every colour, every gesture, a signature of some unanalysable imaginative essence. (*E*, 140)

The knowledge, then, which can be spoken only in "symbol and metaphor" is that consummate energy of the imagination which will have purified and simplified "all things until they become 'infinite and holy'"; and it is by this process that the imagination intuits and gradually defines the Self.

The Self represents the one perfect symbol the poet can evolve: the selfless image the poet makes of himself. But such a symbol necessarily lies beyond grasp of the intellective or the poetic imagination. When "I draw myself up into the symbol it seems as if I should know all if I could but . . . find everything in the symbol" (*V*, 301). The poet singles out "one image" in a search for wisdom (*E*, 95) but that image, or symbol, comes to signify absolute dissolution of the self as an object and as an object-oriented form of consciousness.

So long as art presupposes, then, a need to create, any attempt to symbolize a transpersonal state of mind cannot help but become an art of symbolic paradox. As R. P. Blackmur would say, all profound art is "the gesture of our uncreated selves." [8] It is not strange then that the art of paradox should underlie the mature Yeats's view of tragedy: a Sisyphean but progressive self-renewal in the wake of continual defeat. The heuristic substitute for creative perfection—a symbol of the Self in the making—holds perpetually in suspense the life mystery in which the poet can believe, the one object to which he could be continually drawn in his increasingly more lucid spiritual and poetic correspondence with reality.[9]

The ultimate reality is a moment in which antinomies in human experience dissolve (*V*, 193). The result is an absolute, transpersonal Self-awareness. But that moment, like Blake's intrinsic pulse-beat beyond time, is the felt grasp of an eternal reality rather than that reality itself and constitutes the means by which the visionary life is lived. That life is a symbolic reordering of experience. The poet, Yeats remarked, "is never the bundle of accident and incoherence that sits down to breakfast; he has been reborn as an idea." "He must die every day he lives." And the product of poesis, if too intense for everyday life, nonetheless serves as the gauge of a man's spiritual transformation within its temporal limits. "As I look backward upon my own writing," he says in *Hodos Chameliontos*, "I take pleasure alone in those verses where it seems to me I have found something hard and cold, some articulation of the Image, which is the opposite of all that I am in my daily life." Yet the poet "can no more make this Mask or Image than the seed can be made by the soil into which it is cast" (*A*, 184).

That the self *may* be made over into its ultimate image is the poet's credo. And though the aim of Yeats's poetic search is to shear the mind, the imagination, or the poem of forms or images that do not weave into the poet's ultimate image, his poetry cannot be said therefore "to disintegrate or to circumvent the image in the illusory pursuit of essence," as Allen Tate claims the angelic imagination does when it trespasses the bounds of the "symbolic imagination.[10] "The deep truth is imageless," as Shelley has Demogorgon declare, but to the symbolic imagination, Tate points out, final disappearance of the image (Beatrice's transfiguration in *Paradiso* is Tate's example) becomes the point of spiritual incarnation, the moment the image, the word, the vision is wholly internalized.[11]

The poem may be felt becoming a form of incarnation when our attention to images is made to give way to an awareness of the "Ghostly Voice," or daimonic presence, in the poetry. Discussion in the following chapters is arranged to offer a reading of six groups of Yeats's poems, relative to six key poems which most dynamically illustrate Yeats's heuristic belief in a ghostly presence. I have assumed throughout that the speaking voice and not the image is the primary force in each poem,[12] and that the flow of images in the poetry as a whole is toward articulation of the invisible image, or symbol, of the speaker's daimonic Self. The speaker's inherent concern, in the overall direction of the poetry, is to exercise his spiritual imagination so as to be rid of all antithetical awareness: of contrary ideas, images and things reified and separated by a myopic response to life.

In Chapter 2 three early poems are compared to the late revision of an early poem, "The Lamentation of the Old Pensioner." The speaker's gradual mastery over temporal and topographical referents appears to challenge the dualistic bias underlying those poems. Chapter 3 is concerned with the poet's contrary image of the beloved and the speaker's uneasy alternation in addressing himself both to an idealized and to a sensuous form of love. The love poems of *The Wind Among the Reeds* are seen in relation to Yeats's dream poem "The Cap and Bells" and then to the first "realistic" love poems, "He hears the Cry of the Sedge" and "He reproves the Curlew." The marital love poems, representing Yeats's middle period, are examined in Chapter 4 in relation to "The Gift of Harun Al-Raschid." "The Gift of Harun Al-Raschid" is the first of the love poems in which a daimonic image appears in the likeness of the Self-oriented hero, forecasting a change in attitude of the speaker to his conflicting images of the beloved.

The poems discussed in Chapter 5 begin to reveal the speaker as the prime beneficiary of his daimonic intelligence. The deepening of expressive energy in the speaker's voice increases from the heroic Helen poems, to the poems of exultation ("The Dawn," "Tom O'Roughley"), to what may be called the "stigmatic" poems of exultation ("The Cold Heaven," "Demon and Beast"). With their heightened emphasis on insight through pain or suffering, the "stigmatic" poems anticipate the Yeatsian speaker's most characteristic voice—his expression of "tragic joy." The terminal point of reference for the poems examined in this chapter is "The Second Coming." Analysis of the symbolic intensity of "The Second Coming" prepares in Chapter 6 for consideration of related poems dealing with the theme of destruction. And here, various propositions about the biographical, social, spiritual, and mythic underpinnings of the love poetry and the poetry of exultation are explored through a "psychopoetic analysis" of "Leda and the Swan."

This study concludes with examination of the comparative organicity of the culminating image in memorable poems of Yeats's last period— "Among School Children," "Byzantium," and "Lapis Lazuli." The antithetical intensity of the late poems and of Yeats's body of poetry as a whole are seen in relation to two poems written within a year of his death—"The Circus Animals' Desertion" and "High Talk." Here, more successfully than in preceding poems, poetic imagery is made subordinate to the integrity of the speaking voice. The two poems best illustrate the contrary impulse of Yeats's poetic energies: toward an ever more lambent expression of self-liberation and toward a more profoundly realistic expression of self-disillusionment. If image and idea were ever progenitors of poetry they must finally leave in control of the poem the passionate tension of the speaking voice. The biopolarity of the creative life, and Yeats's vacillating concern with love, Self, and world thus make of the poetry an open dialogue, purposively designed to project the increasing rigor of the speaker's dialectical sensibility.

chapter 2

the transvaluation of time and place:
four poems reflecting Yeats's spiritual-esthetic development

In 1931 Yeats, looking back over his career, claimed that a man is forced to choose between "perfection of the life" and perfection "of the work" (*P,* 495). In contrast, for example, to his extroverted contemporary Oscar Wilde, Yeats fairly early in his career chose perfection "of the work." His efforts as a poet were spent shaping ideas and feelings into art: not because that was a substitute for life, but because the poem, as he conceived it, was meant to give a heightened sense of life—embodying a perfection always just beyond his immediate stage of comprehension. For this reason the poem was to Yeats as a lure and guide to the continual refinement of his perceptual and poetic sensibility.

The poem for Yeats was demonstration of an inner discipline, serving both as an esthetic and as a spiritual vehicle. As T. S. Eliot had argued, and critics like Donald Stauffer and Richard Ellmann actually have shown, Yeats's poetry as a whole becomes more comprehensible when regarded as an organic continuum. And this certainly accords with the way Yeats liked to regard his work. It is true that he would have been little more than a significant minor poet had he stopped writing after 1900; but it is equally true that what he wrote after 1900 did not come about of itself.[1] His evolution from a nineteenth- to a twentieth-century poet was the result of a continuous change in style and point of view—a bilateral development which testifies to the growth of his spiritual imagination.

A close examination of two early poems and two late revisions of early poems suggests that the development in Yeats's poetry comes about through a gradual marriage of the creative and the spiritual processes. This has usually been assumed to be the overall organizing principle in Yeats's poetry, but it has not been sufficiently explored as a formative principle in the individual poems.

I propose to study in four poems what John Hall Wheelock has called the "fourth voice" in poetry, an articulate energy addressed to "some older wiser Self in which all selves are included." [2] We may call this the "speaking voice" and use the term to suggest an ultimate identity between Self-realization and creative self-expression. The speaking voice is an intrinsic force in the poem which can so transform images that we come to recognize the person of the speaker as the real subject of the poem. [3]

My analysis will be drawn from a reading of "The Lake Isle of Innisfree," "The Two Trees," "The Dedication to a Book of Stories selected from the Irish Novelists," and "The Lamentation of the Old Pensioner."

"The Lake Isle of Innisfree," Yeats tells us, was written in London; it was composed in the winter of 1888 and reflects a young man's nostalgic memories of summer haunts he frequented as a child living in Sligo. [4] His intention in the poem, as he told Katharine Tynan, was to draw on an already familiar world of imaginative experience, and to get away from the charming but artificial dream world of Indians and fauns. He wanted somehow to "substitute the feelings and longings of nature for those of art" (*KT*, 76–77).

In "The Lake Isle" Yeats expresses the "longings of nature" through his first significant use in poetry of the speaking voice. The physical setting in the poem is the Irishman's Walden, very modestly outfitted by the wishful thinking of the speaker:

[1] I will arise and go now, and go to Innisfree,
[2] And a small cabin build there, of clay and wattles made:
[3] Nine bean-rows will I have there, a hive for the honey-bee,
[4] And live alone in the bee-loud glade.

The island in Lough Gill that is known as Innisfree is actually too small to afford room for a glade, but this need not have deterred the speaker in the poem. He imagines the world he describes.

Underlying the succession of visual images in the opening stanza is a sonantal and rhythmic counterpoint. Front and back vowels vie with each other; there is an interplay of ascending and descending, or retarding, rhythms. The opening half-line, "I will arise and go now," with its heavy emphasis on the long *e*'s (or *i*'s) and *o*'s, moves in a retarding meter, in spite of the fact that the sense of the words themselves tries to move the line forward. The second half of the line—"and go to Innisfree"—moves unequivocably in ascending meter.

It is curious, too, that the sonantal, no less than the rhythmic, pattern contradicts the apparent sense of line one. The meaning of the first three words—"I will arise"—is appropriately echoed by a sequence of three upper front vowels, *e* or *i;* and by way of reinforcement the line terminates with a sequence of front vowels. But what are we to make of the four intervening upper back vowel sounds, *o* or *oo?* Certainly the words of which they are part—"go now . . . go to"—suggest physical movement, but the *o-oo*'s themselves reverberate as though being savored by the speaker in restless reverie. If we have in mind what finally happens in the last stanza, where the *o* sound and the aural (rather than kinetic) image predominate, then we will come to regard the picture summoned up in the first line, and in the three lines which follow, as more emblematic than actual.

The retarding of the movement of line is brought about in each of the next three lines of the poem (2 to 4) by an ambivalent stress pattern: "small cabin build there," "nine bean-rows," "bee-loud glade." There is more than a casual reference to each of the three images named, and yet we are left undecided as to what element in each of the three image phrases is to be stressed most. As a result one tends to pause over the several syllables in each phrase.[5] There is a further slowing down of movement as a result of the shortening of the final line in the stanza (a pattern repeated in each of the following two stanzas). And a further factor contributing to this slowing of pace is the sequence of long-vowel sounds in the terminating three syllables of the stanza: "bee-loud glade."

The emphasis on physical detail in the first three lines, with their predominance of front-vowel sounds, draws our attention to the visual image, the object as it would seem to exist "out there." The last three words, "bee-loud glade," encourage, however, an auditory rather than a visual response. The less definite sound effect thus seems to have entered into competition with the more specific visual effect. The back-vowels *o-oo*, which were first used in line one in words denoting time and movement, in line four become associated with images of sound and solitude.

We may feel then the ear, as well as the eye, being brought into play.

with a corresponding sense of being drawn back, rather than forward, as we follow through the sequence of images in the stanza.

By amplifying the image, Yeats claimed, increasing by ambiguity its range of reference, "any highly subjective art can escape from the barrenness and shallowness of a too conscious arrangement, into the abundance and depth of Nature" (*E*, 87). In "The Lake Isle" the images of nature are made progressively less definite, enabling the picture we are given of Innisfree to become concentrated finally into an image having symbolic significance. A sense of mystery begins to inform the images in stanza 2 of the poem, so that not only does the visual image become less tangible, but the visible form tends to fuse with the aural impression:

[5] And I shall have some peace there, for peace comes dropping slow,
[6] Dropping from the veils of the morning to where the cricket sings;
[7] There midnight's all a glimmer, and noon a purple glow,
[8] And evening full of the linnet's wings.

We are not sure what we are meant to see, and what we are meant to hear. The peculiar phrasing in line 5 treats the idea of "peace" as though it was something liquid, and again, stress on the word "dropping" superimposes upon the normally iambic phrase following the caesura a descending meter: "for / peáce comes / drópping / slów" (cf. line 1, stanza 1). For the first time the diphthongal *o-oo* sound assumes a strategic place in the line, and this might possibly induce us to read the final words as an auditory image. A reading of the next line (6) establishes the retarding effect of the word "dropping" and identifies with this effect the sound image both at the beginning and at the end of that line; the midsection of the line demonstrates the reverse pattern, an ascending meter with the suggestion of a visual image:

[6] Drópping/ from the veíls/ of the mórning// to whére/ the crícket/ síngs. . . .

The word "veils" may possibly refer to morning mist;[6] at any rate it is meant to convey an impression less definite, more mysterious and evanescent, than any of the visual impressions conveyed by images in stanza 1.

The back vowel *o* has a dominant position in the first half of line 6, while the front vowels *e-i* dominate in the second half. The *e-i* seem identified here with an auditory image, giving a virtually onomatopoetic effect to the words, "cricket sings."

In the first half of line 7 it is the frontal *e-i* sounds which dominate, while in the second half it is the back *o-oo* sounds: just the reverse of line 6. The images described in the line are entirely visual, but they give the impression of something airy, indefinite in contour—the shimmering and diffusive qualities of light and color.[7] In line 8 the ambiguity increases so that it is difficult to say whether the impression we get of the image is visual or aural. Once more the front vowels (which in stanza 1 were associated with the physical or the visual image) dominate, but the rhyme scheme "cricket sings"—"linnet's wings" might very well carry over from line 6 the impression of something heard. After all, we are left in doubt as to whether it is early or late "evening," and so are we to suppose the speaker actually sees, or can he only hear, the flutter of the linnet's wings?

By the final stanza the visual impression of the island is almost totally eclipsed by the dominance of images of sound. Concomitantly the quickening effect that the speaker's eagerness has upon the movement of the line is checked by a deepening stress put on the back vowels, which go primarily into the making up of auditory images:

> [9] I will arise and go now, for always night and day
> [10] I hear lake water lapping with low sounds by the shore;
> [11] While I stand on the roadway, or on the pavements grey,
> [12] I hear it in the deep heart's core.

Again, as in the earlier stanzas, the lines here reveal the tension between back and front vowels. In lines 9 and 11 the *e-i* sounds (at the beginning and at the end of the line) enclose the *o-oo* sounds; while in lines 10 and 12 the *o* sounds dominate because they constitute the strategic rhyme sound at the end. The sound pattern thus serves to reinforce the tension between both the visual and auditory images as well as the tension between the forward and retarding rhythms in the stanza.

In line 10 the emphasis on hearing rather than going induces stress on the first syllables, serving to stay the movement of that line. In line 11 the stress on "while" and "stand" make for a pattern of descending meter, contrasting with the "I will arise" and its overall ascending movement in line 9. There is a consequent paling (through generalizing) of the physical image in line 11—"on the roadway, or on the pavements grey"—as though in preparation for the culminating internalized image "I hear it in the deep heart's core." As in stanza 1 the shortening of the final line draws increased attention to the last three syllables, remarkably transposed from the identical words in Blake's poem "The Smile."

The effect those last syllables have in Yeats's poem is unique. The direction of the sounds recapitulates the sonantal progression in the poem as a whole. The *e–a–o* sequence echoes the change from a front to a middle to a back vowel, and this progression inward, so marked in these climactic words, caps the emphasis put in the poem on the auditory rather than the visual image. And because the auditory emphasis points to an intangible location for the Isle of Innisfree, the latter takes on symbolic meaning.

"The Lake Isle" thus provides a unique sonantal and rhythmic basis for the symbolizing process. As Yeats said, looking back over his work in 1922, the poem was "my first lyric with anything in its rhythm of my own music" (*A*, 103). Yeats had to work toward making the speaking voice reflect the flow and concentration of imaginative energy, as description of the isle found the way to its symbolic center. The peace and solitude which the island finally signifies, however, cannot be defined in terms of time or place; the image of Innisfree represents, rather, a wishful mood, a state of unconscious longing. In probing the imaginative depths of his subject the speaker appears to desire an undefinable freedom and a means to express that freedom.

Idea and image do not finally enjoy an independent existence in the poem but point instead to the meditative presence of the speaker. As Yeats puts it describing the intention of his poetic drama, image and idea are meant to become lost "in patterns of sound, as the name of God is lost in Arabian arabesques" [8] and the art which accomplishes this, "while seeming to separate from the world and us a group of figures, images, symbols, enables us to pass for a few moments into a deep of the mind that had hitherto been too subtle for our habitation" (*E*, 225). What the self is becomes clear only to the extent that the mind is able to sink in on reality and move toward an understanding of the being that underlies the multiplicity of forms existing outside. The unconscious Self is brought toward the threshold of consciousness in the degree that the speaker is able to reflect, rather than to desire (or be embittered by), things outside. In this way, if we may project the process described in "The Lake Isle," the speaker as lover will later be able to relate to, without actually possessing, his Beloved; and similarly, in a more public role the speaker will be able to entertain his vision of reality without being offended or deterred by the persistent blindness or hostility of the audience he may be addressing.

In "The Lake Isle" the temporal world, of men and cities, is obviously what the speaker is reacting against, but we are given only the barest glimpse of that world. This presumably is because a more explicit view would disturb the idyllic or contemplative mood that the speaker is trying to create. Looking back thirty years later, Yeats claimed that the originality of his "Lake Isle" consisted in his ability to "escape from rhetoric and from that emotion of the crowd that rhetoric brings" (*A*, 103).

But leaving behind the crowd, if that is what Yeats actually had in mind, resulted in a not altogether perfect creation. "The Lake Isle" later embarrassed the poet because of its archaic phrasing (ll. 1, 9, 11) and its disregard of "the common syntax." What was necessary if Yeats's language was to become entirely his own was his further "loosening" of the poetic rhythm, so that the intensity of the spoken word would fill in, and tighten, the line. This meant that the poet would have to extend himself sufficiently to make "public" his speech (as Archibald MacLeish has said[9]), accounting more fully in the poetry for the adverse reality of the everyday world. It is Yeats's quarrel with the real world that over the years helped to intensify his poetry and helped to broaden the range of the speaking voice in his poems.

We may consider the extent of Yeats's development by sketching very briefly some biographical background and then by looking at one more early poem and after that two late revisions of early poems—focusing on what threatens to stand in the way of the poet's total realization of an unconscious, transpersonal Self: the unavoidable, and necessarily human, response he must make to the world about him (*A*, 235–36). In examining the poems we shall find that we are dealing with essentially the same phenomenon we dealt with in "The Lake Isle"—the means by which the speaking voice assimilates images of an externalized reality.

It was Maud Gonne who first made the real world a factor in Yeats's poetry.[10] For this reason 1889, the year he met Maud, was a turning point in his career. The volume which he published in January of that year, *The Wanderings of Oisin and other Poems,* had only limited reference to experiences which transpired outside the realm of pure imagination. Until that time, too, he had been especially interested in the occult, and his membership in the Hermetic, the Golden Dawn, and the Theosophical societies helped insulate his mind from what he considered the distraction of city life. Shortly after he was introduced to Maud, the latter persuaded Yeats to capitalize on his interest in the theater and write a play that would rally national sentiments in Dublin. The result was Yeats's first Irish verse play, *The Countess Cathleen.*

Yeats had in mind the subject of his play for some time before he met Maud Gonne, but now he had ample reason for getting down to the writing of it. There was real provocation, for he could comment on idealist sentiments, inspired by the example of more than a mythical heroine. Cathleen, the legendary prototype of Maud Gonne, was a noble woman who would give even her soul to relieve the poverty of the Irish peasant. Maud herself was absolutely committed to the cause of Ireland, and though Yeats was struck by the nobleness and persistence of her convictions, he could not help but turn mentor. From the very beginning he expressed concern for her naïvete, and his ambiguous treatment of Countess Cathleen's idealism seems to reflect his disapproving attitude toward Maud's radical idealism.[11] At the same time, however, the exuberant charm of this young woman served as a catalyst for Yeats's deeper involvement in the Irish Renaissance. And no matter whether it was sympathy or antipathy, his new awareness of the "world of action" in Ireland could no longer be kept out of his writing.

By 1891 Yeats was weaned from too exclusive an interest in the mysteries of the imagination and found himself taking a more vital part in the new cultural and political movement. Although he would never surrender his identity to a public program of any kind, Yeats did respond to the spirit of the times and became (what George Moore ironically called) "the great founder." In 1891 and 1892 he formed three literary groups, the Rhymers' Club and the Irish Literary Society in London, and the Irish Literary Society in Dublin. His interest in the esoteric and the occult was gradually converted to the province of literature—and, in particular, to what in literature was eminently Irish.

With this we can return to the poetry and focus our attention on three poems first published between 1890 and 1892: "The Two Trees," "Dedication to a Book of Stories," and "The Lamentation of the Old Pensioner." The poems appeared together, in close sequence, in Yeats's second volume of verse *The Countess Cathleen and Various Legends and Lyrics* (1892).

Maud Gonne confided to Virginia Moore that "The Two Trees" was her favorite poem by Yeats,[12] and it is quite obvious that Yeats wrote the poem with Maud Gonne in mind.

The speaker in "The Two Trees" addresses his beloved, advising her not to look beyond herself for the source of happiness: "Beloved gaze in thine own heart, / The holy tree is growing there." As is generally recognized, Yeats appropriated for his central image an esoteric symbol, the cabalistic tree of good and evil, innocence and knowledge, life and death.[13] The image comes into the poem already charged with its old associations so that the speaker simply elaborates: not using the occasion as a stepping stone to some memorable revelation, as in "The Lake Isle," but coming full circle to the initial proposition. The poem reads as a moral lesson and is skillfully worded, neatly balanced, tightly structured.[14]

The speaker seems entirely self-assured, as though he might have just emerged from his study of ancient wisdom, illuminated by his desire to apply his knowledge of the heart and the world. In the first half of the discourse he extends the metaphor of "the holy tree" to indicate his harmony with nature, and to suggest the self-evident truth of his own vision:

> The shaking of its leafy head
> Has given the waves their melody,
> And made my lips and music wed,
> Murmuring a wizard song for thee.

The vision reveals the speaker's stake in the beloved's understanding of herself:

> There the Loves a circle go,
> The flaming circle of our days,
> Gyring, spiring to and fro
> In those great ignorant leafy ways;
> Remembering all that shaken hair
> And how the wingèd sandals dart,
> Thine eyes grow full of tender care:
> Beloved, gaze in thine own heart.

It would seem this speaker is reminding the beloved of the sacred realm of the imagination, referring perhaps to the ideal situation of immortal lovers. The most he can do, however, without disclosing his own feelings, is call the beloved back from whatever engages her in the external world. But the urgency of his warning is not quite as evident here as it is in "The Poet pleads with the Elemental Powers," a poem written just a few months later:

> Great powers of falling wave and wind and windy fire,
> With your harmonious choir
> Encircle her I love and sing her into peace,
> That my old care may cease;
> Unfold your flaming wings and cover out of sight
> The nets of day and night.

Although the speaker in "The Two Trees" somewhat emerges from the embracing "we" of poems concerned with idyllic love (for example, "The Indian to his Love," "The White Birds"), it is evident that he still holds to the possibility of a unitive relationship with the beloved. In this connection the elaboration of the central image in the poem seems almost magical, as though its unifying power in itself provided a nostrum against the disruptive evil which existed outside. The image of the tree thus takes dominant hold of the poem, precluding any vigorous projection of the speaking voice. In "The Poet pleads," on the other hand, the speaker contends with the "Great Powers" which he invokes to protect his beloved, and in the end would seem to approach closer to the source of their influence:

> Dim Powers of drowsy thought, let her no longer be
> Like the pale cup of the sea. . . .
> . . . .
> But let a gentle silence wrought with music flow
> Whither her footsteps go.

The image of the "Great Powers" is more mysterious than the image of the "tree" because it is less definite, less cerebral, and less magical, in its conception: as a result the speaking voice comes to be more evident in the poem as a transforming power in its own right—extracting from the image of a seemingly physical force the corresponding image of that force internalized. The Huntian allusion to "drowsy thought" and "gentle silence" thus serves to invert the reference to any external reality.

The "Dim Powers of drowsy thought," the image on which the sense of "The Poet pleads" turns, describes the potential the speaker has for transforming his subject. The image appears also to be what the speaker in "The Two Trees" has in mind when he tells the beloved: "gaze in thine own heart, / The holy tree is growing there." The only transformation of reality, he seems to say, takes place internally. The "fatal image," on the other hand, "grows" outside the bounds of imagination, and can only stifle, not enhance, the recreative power of the mind:

> . . . all things turn to barrenness
> In the dim glass the demons hold,
> The glass of outer weariness,
> Made when God slept in times of old.
> There, through the broken branches, go
> The ravens of unresting thought;
> Flying, crying, to and fro,
> Cruel claw and hungry throat. . . .

The "dim glass" only dissipates the "Powers of . . . thought," reflecting a world which is destructive because it is without direction, without the concentrated energy of intellect or imagination.

The "ravens of unresting thought" anticipate the divided images in "The Second Coming," the uncontrolled "falcon" and the ineffectual "desert birds." And as in another late poem, "Demon and Beast," in "The Two Trees" the central image (of the "tree") depicts the daimonic and the demonic imagination as mirror opposites.[15] In stanza 1 of the poem the daimonic (or spiritual) imagination is identified with an inward-awareness, while in stanza 2 the demonic imagination is represented as devoid of any human or spiritual center. Instead of the concentric, resolving development of image in the first stanza, we have in stanza 2 an unsettling, centrifugal, sequence of poetic images. However, through the final, negative command in the poem, "Gaze no more in the bitter glass," the speaker indirectly urges the beloved to "gaze" once more "in thine own heart."

In 1917 Yeats stated what he felt was the reason for writing poetry: "One goes on year after year getting the disorder of one's mind in order, and this is the real impulse to create" (*L,* 627). We can say that Yeats's most memorable poetry results from the continual re-forming of the speaker's view of reality, clarifying, reconciling and finally dissolving conflicting emotions and opposed states of mind.

The poem, Yeats felt, insofar as it takes form on paper, reflects the paradox of the spiritual-esthetic experience: "I have always felt that the soul has two movements primarily: one to transcend forms, and the other to create forms" (*L,* 403). How to merge effectively these contrary motives was Yeats's principal artistic concern. It is in the late poems (e.g. "Byzantium," "Lapis Lazuli," "High Talk") that we see the end result of his search—the attempt of the speaker to realize a unified view of reality while allowing him to transcend the verbal limitations of the poem. In the early poems, especially the two which we shall consider now, we see the raw materials for the evolution of this imaginative process. In considering these early poems we have also the advantage of observing how the poet radically rewrites the early material, bringing it into line with his later, more fully developed, idea about the function of art.

"The Dedication to a Book of Stories" concerns itself more than either poem we have dealt with thus far with the relation of the speaker to the external world. Though "The Dedication" is most akin to "The Two Trees" it differs from that poem in that it offers not a dualistic but an integrated point of view.

Instead of a clearcut division between the two halves of "The Dedication" there is a continuity of development in the progression from the first to the second half of the poem. In the first twelve lines the speaker tells of a talisman from nature whose power to heal is presumed to have been lost with the passing of the Celtic world-view: "a green branch hung with many a bell / When her own people ruled tragic Eire." Its magical influence

> . . . charmed away the merchant from his guile,
> And turned the farmer's memory from his cattle,
> And hushed in sleep the roaring ranks of battle:
> And all grew friendly for a little while.

The speaker in *The Wanderings of Oisin* makes reference some half-dozen times to the possible transforming influence of the branch, but in that earlier narrative the magic charm remains in the realm of faery, of little avail to the hero who chooses to return to this world: " 'O wandering Oisin, the strength of the bell-branch is naught, / For there moves alive in your fingers the fluttering sadness of earth' "(*P*, 55). In "The Dedication" (ll. 13–24), in contrast, the speaker claims the power of the Celtic talisman. The speaking voice, as it were, appropriates the object and makes it an instrument of the imagination.

To be sure, in lines 17–20 the object reasserts itself as an ambivalent and independent image of joy and release, eclipsing the formative power of the speaking voice; in lines 21–24, however, the image of the "bells" is made secondary and the speaking voice once more comes into its own.

We become aware finally that it is the transforming spirit of the speaker's imagination, and not the proliferating image of the "green boughs" which determines the process of the poem. Unlike the cabalistic central symbol in "The Two Trees," the Celtic symbol in "The Dedication" becomes transmuted, absorbed into a train of images which describes jointly the barren spirit of Ireland and the redeeming state of mind of the speaker. The speaking voice thus appears to resolve by attempting to synthesize conflicting moods:

[12] . . . I also bear a bell-branch full of ease.

[13] I tore it from green boughs winds tore and tossed
[14] Until the sap of summer had grown weary!
[15] I tore it from the barren boughs of Eire,
[16] That country where a man can be so crossed;

[17] Can be so battered, badgered and destroyed
[18] That he's a loveless man; gay bells bring laughter
[19] That shakes a mouldering cobweb from the rafter;
[20] And yet the saddest chimes are best enjoyed.

[21] Gay bells or sad, they bring you memories
[22] Of half-forgotten innocent old places:
[23] We and our bitterness have left no traces
[24] On Munster grass and Connemara skies.

The metaphorical "I tore it from the green boughs" sets the tone from line 12 on: it is the most striking example of the energy with which the speaking voice informs the poem. Stanzas 4 through 6 then proceed to describe the change that can occur given the controlling force of the imagination. By juxtaposing contrary elements—"green boughs," "barren boughs" / "gay bells," "sad . . . chimes"—the speaker recalls the past and attempts to make it present to the mind's eye. In the process he revitalizes "our" sense of time and place, and attributes to our ability to contain conflicting emotions a related capacity for recapturing our original, "innocent" feelings. It is the bitterness of personal experience that makes the world seem barren, the scattered pieces of a dark, demonic imagination.

Unlike his counterpart in "The Two Trees" the speaker in "The Dedication" is not content with simply describing the "broken boughs" as an epitome of "things turn[ed] to barrenness." He tries to synthesize from the representation of two opposing views of "things" a disciplined, even-tempered, response to the world, a response that sympathetically reflects the human condition. In this way the speaker himself seems to be setting an example.

Yeats's revision in 1924 of lines 20–24 is what makes "The Dedication" turn out to be a dialectic of the imagination. The paradox in line 20; the transition from an image-centered to an imagination-centered response to the past, lines 21–22; and the clear differentiation in lines 23–24 between the subjective and the objective reality—all derive from a sharper, more resilient, and immediate quality in the speaking voice. The original lines, in comparison, seem sentimental in tone and only awkwardly in the last line suggest a rallying point from the poem's nostalgic referral to the past:

[20] The sad bells bow the forehead on the hands.

[21] A honied ringing! under the new skies
[22] They bring you memories of old village faces,
[23] Cabins gone now, old well-sides, old dear places,
[24] And men who loved the cause that never dies.

The ending of this 1891 version of "The Dedication" may have an emotional or rhetorical appeal, but the abrupt transition in time-sense does not allow in these lines for an effective poetic tension. The original is improved on in that, in the rewriting, the introversion of image and point of view more conspicuously emphasizes the role of the imagination, as it is projected through the speaking voice.[16]

"The Lamentation of the Old Pensioner" has been more radically revised than "The Dedication." The later poem contains none of the original lines or phrases, and even adds to the original two a third—middle—stanza. As Thomas Parkinson, the first to deal extensively with this poem, notes, the later version of "The Old Pensioner" is "the logical outcome of Yeats's final revisions, the end toward which all the other revisions [i.e., in other early poems] were straining."[17] The later version seems to be virtually a different poem, characteristic of Yeats's later style. For no apparent reason, one might suppose, it was retained under the original title in new editions of the early volume, *The Countess Cathleen and Various Legends and Lyrics* (1892; incorporated in editions of Yeats's poetry since 1895 under the heading, *The Rose*).

Yeats wrote his first publisher of "The Old Pensioner" that the poem

was "an almost verbatim record of words by an old Irishman" (*L,* 158).
The poem is a lament for what is obviously beyond the speaker's control, the change in the world about him. The narrator merely voices regret for "the old days long gone by." As a young man in his early twenties, Yeats had become interested in country people who preserved their
old ways and customs, and might have wanted to have this record of an
"old Irishman" simply because of the fascination with the past that, in
various ways, prevailed throughout his own life. But it turned out that
when Yeats himself was approaching old age, he could abide only a
tough-minded attitude to the inevitable lure of the past. As a result,
without changing the title or the subject of this poem (an old man's
memories), he might quite possibly have been impelled to show the
transformation in his own mind; and so he completely undid the senti-
mentality evident in the early work, substituting for it the bristling tone
of his later style. The early poem itself must have been the occasion for
the later poem, touching off in the poet a need to overhaul, as though in
answer to, the person of the narrator in the original version.

It is no wonder then that "The Old Pensioner" shows more fire, offering a more strenuous report of the imagination than the three early
poems we have already considered. Unlike the previous poems "The
Old Pensioner" focuses squarely upon the change that has come about
in the person of the speaker with respect to the things referred to by images used in the poem.

If we compare the later version with the original we see to what degree the speaker in "The Old Pensioner" has come to hold his own.
Here, side by side, are the 1890 and 1925 versions:

I had a chair at every hearth,	[1] Although I shelter from the rain
When no one turned to see	[2] Under a broken tree
With 'Look at the old fellow there;	[3] My chair was nearest to the fire
And who may he be?'	[4] In every company
And therefore do I wander on,	[5] That talked of love or politics,
And the fret is on me.	[6] Ere Time transfigured me.
	[7] Though lads are making pikes again
	[8] For some conspiracy,
	[9] And crazy rascals rage their fill
	[10] At human tyranny,
	[11] My contemplations are of Time
	[12] That has transfigured me.

The road-side trees keep mur-	[13] There's not a woman turns her face
muring—	
Ah, wherefore murmur ye	[14] Upon a broken tree,
As in the old days long gone	[15] And yet the beauties that I loved
by,	
Green oak and poplar tree!	[16] Are in my memory;
The well-known faces are all	[17] I spit into the face of Time
gone,	
And the fret is on me.	[18] That has transfigured me.

The sentimental tone of the speaker is what weakens his position in the poem written in 1890. He appears as a fretful wanderer lost in the world which surrounds him. He is a victim, and in no way a beneficiary, of Time. In the later poem the speaker stations himself at the center, contemplating, and by this means rising above, his particular experience of life. The world around him and time itself serve, he claims, for his own transfiguration.

The speaker in the later version of "The Old Pensioner" dwells only in a passing way on each image, the recall of the past used deliberately to intensify his present awareness. The images become as successive springboards for the final, cumulative response of the speaker to what he contemplates; and as a result the climax of the poem depends upon the shift in emphasis (ll. 16–18) from the three stanza train of temporal images to the startling imaginative energy of the speaker asserting he has moved beyond all restrictions of time.

As Parkinson pointed out, the final "transfigured me" takes us so by surprise that it seems fairly to "leap from the page."[18] The surprise, however, has been adequately prepared for through the verbal development of the poem.

By the end of "The Old Pensioner" we become aware that the imaginal line is drawn between "Time" and "me." The difference between these two terms seems intentionally pointed up through a pyramiding of images of opposite intent. Thus the pronominal forms "I," "my," and "me" (used a total of nine times in the three stanzas) are used in contrast with object nouns such as "rain," "fire," "pikes," "rascals," and "broken tree." The sequence converges upon a return to the original picture of the narrator sheltering himself from the rain under a broken tree, but with his self-sufficiency now established: "I spit into the face of Time." The image of external things, bad weather, and foul politics, in this way is countered by a gesture of defiance, vigorously asserting the speaker's integrity.

The only significant element retained from the original version of the poem is the persistent *e* rhyme. In the later version the emphasis on the *e* sound is redoubled by the use of the long or short *i* in the terminal syllable of all but one of the unrhymed lines. The result is that the images of time and transfiguration are molded into such a pattern of close opposition that the one, finally, becomes absorbed into the other: "Time" is the one inclusive image for those terminal word-images in the unrhymed lines, but its summary placement in the next to last line of the poem is sonantally ironic, being sandwiched in between the culminating rhyme words (ll. 17 and 18) which firmly establish in the poem an internalized point of view.

Thus, sonantally, verbally, and thematically the progression is toward an effective statement of the use to which the spiritual imagination is put. The poem has a soritical logic in that the successive alternation between opposing images works to reflect back on the initial "I" in line one: and this in turn, by the final three lines, intensifies the emphasis put on the "I" as the single, transformed image in the poem.

It is interesting that the narrator in the poem should associate politics and love, and that his penultimate statement should attempt to immortalize "the beauties that I loved" by assigning them an inviolable place in his memory. The narrator reminds himself of Ireland's time of troubles, and at the same time seems intent on preserving from that bitter reminder his image of the woman he loved. She appears, in her ideal form, to share in the glory of his own transfiguration. We of course may call to mind the ideal love-image Yeats himself retained of Maud Gonne, whose political activities he quite disapproved of.

The image of the "broken tree" ambiguously relates both to the outside world ("There's not a woman turns her face / Upon a broken tree" —ll. 13–14) and to the private world where the old man takes shelter (ll. 1–2). It perhaps reminds us of the dendrological symbol of "the broken branches" in "The Two Trees" as well as of the magical symbol of the "bell-branch" in "The Dedication." [19] In "The Old Pensioner," however, the "broken tree" is one of a number of images of a natural or physical object which have been filtered through the imagination, and are used now to show the pervading intensity of the speaking voice. As a result the image of the tree necessarily lacks the force of a dominating symbol. If there is any developed symbol in the poem, it is that of the "I"—a projection of the speaker's formidable awareness of the metamorphosed self.

Of the four poems we have treated here "The Old Pensioner" most clearly shows the speaker in the process of emerging toward a passionate Self-awareness. The lonely figure of the old man is distinguished from the figure of the lover in "The Two Trees" in that the former's love is self-sufficient, seemingly independent of the people, the circumstances, and the physical world around him; and similarly, he is distinguished from the solitary speaker in "The Lake Isle" and "The Dedication" in that from the very beginning the perspicuous quality of his voice pervades the imagery in the poem, unequivocably establishing him as the principal figure and subject of the poem.

The two early poems and two related late poems discussed here show a progression that is characteristic of Yeats's poetry as a whole, from his early to his late period. The poet's heuristic belief in a transpersonal Self, which is fully expressed only in his late period, is operative in the early work in that it gradually determines the emergence of the speaking voice as a dominant force in the poem. The later version of the early lyric, "The Old Pensioner," shows the logical course of this poetic development.

Some basis has been established then for viewing Yeats's poetry as an imaginative progression toward a spiritual objective. What serves to sharpen the language, reshape the imagery, tighten the syntactic structure, and intensify feeling in the individual poem is the projection (through the speaking voice) of the poet's increasing consciousness of a daimonic sensibility—the creative detachment by which the poem transforms its speaker's grating awareness of the everyday world.

"love's lonely hour":
spiritual conflict in the wind among the reeds

In "The Old Pensioner" we have an instance of that saving power peculiar to Yeats's later poetry, the ability of the speaker to suggest by his own response to the changing world around him some vital, unassailable still-point in time. By contrast, in the early love poetry of *The Rose* and *The Wind Among the Reeds* Yeats attempts to depict a still-point beyond time, a realm of truth and beauty apocalyptically conceived. The speaker, very much in the throes of love, is pictured as desiring to throw off every vestige of his own personality in order to dedicate himself entirely to his immortal beloved. He is impatient to be rid of life and to be consumed by something other than himself. But the image of eternal beauty that he projects proves finally beyond the solitary pale of his imagination.

By the time he was twenty-four, just before he met Maud Gonne, Yeats was already well experienced at disestablishing the ascendancy of an extrinsic ideal. He had created his Endymion and his Alastor, and moved beyond them, in *Oisin.* The titular hero of that early but accomplished poem seeks in the unchanging world of the Immortals repose from his restless quest for love, truth, and beauty; Oisin exhausts his desire for a changeless reality and, like an existentialist hero, decides to return to the unsettling conditions of this world, renewing his understanding of and compassion for "the ancient sadness of men."

Yeats's poetry is a record of alternations between the two kinds of reality—"race and soul." He tries to keep in equipoise the double reference of his poetry, and if the spiritual outlook finally dominates, it is made palatable by the poet's consistently humanizing intelligence.

Although Yeats never did surrender his image of the ideal woman— "the trouble of my life," as he said—he begins in his later poetry to welcome the failure of any projected ideal, and to find strength in the magnetic power, vacillating as it may be, of his own independent vision. The image of the rose gradually weakens in view of the mundane reality it purports to displace [1]; and we can perhaps believe that there was built into the early poetry a humanistic safeguard against any Platonizing tendency. In 1925, taking a backward glance at the poems in *The Rose,* Yeats himself supposed there was no question but that "the quality symbolised as The Rose differs from the Intellectual Beauty of Shelley and of Spenser in that I have imagined it as suffering with man and not as something pursued and seen from afar" (*P*, 842).

We shall concern ourselves here with what is generally conceded to be the culminating volume of Yeats's early poetry, *The Wind Among the Reeds.* And we shall begin with analysis of "The Cap and Bells," a key poem which has generally been neglected by Yeats's critics.

Underlying almost all the early love poems is an ironic tension between the speaker's awareness of the real world and his awareness of a higher, spiritual reality. "The Cap and Bells" is unusual in that it is the one memorable poem in the Yeats canon which makes no concession at all to the terrestrial world. Like many another poem it is addressed to the spiritual beloved, the poeticized image of Maud Gonne, but it is an anomaly among the devotional love poems in that it is conceived and beautifully sustained in an ideal world of dream. It shows no trace of irony; and it has nothing of the inhibitive self-consciousness which shows through in other of Yeats's verse.

The uniqueness of "The Cap and Bells" is due to the absence of a real dramatic tension. To be sure, the situation described is sufficiently captivating: the lover is suing for the beloved's hand. But the courtship seems to pursue a predetermined course: the obstacles the lover meets with are only a means to get him to divest himself of any possessive desire, and, by self-sacrifice and personal disembodiment, to finally attain to a state of harmony with the beloved. The tight but fluid structure of the poem convincingly leads us to its inevitable conclusion: depiction of an ultimate peace, safely beyond every manifestation of pain and longing.

Although the poem did not achieve final perfection until the second revision in 1899, Yeats would have us believe that the original pattern for the poem did not change from the moment of its inception.[2] And that moment, the author tells us, derived from, and received elaboration in, the unconscious process of dream. However, it was "more a vision than a dream," Yeats adds, "for it was beautiful and coherent, and gave me the sense of illumination and exaltation that one gets from visions" (*P,* 808).

The delicate, quick-flowing line weaves within the poetic fabric a transparent but imaginatively contained world, making the environment of the poem approach the condition of music. The essential ambiguity of the poem Yeats attributes to its daimonic origin: "The poem has always meant a great deal to me," he said, "though as is the way with symbolic poems, it has not always meant quite the same thing. Blake would have said, 'The authors are in eternity,' and I am quite sure they can only be questioned in dreams" (*P,* 808).

However ambiguous the poem may be, its changing inflection follows quite obviously the course of a spiritual love dialogue; and unlike any other love poem of Yeats this dialogue takes the form of a harmoniously interwoven pattern of gestures.[3]

First we see the lover extend himself to his beloved (he offers up his "soul"). The beloved returns the compliment by coyly turning down the latches of her window. The lover offers his love a second time (he offers her his "heart"). This time the beloved pretends to ignore his gift: "she took up her fan from the table / And waved it [his 'heart'] off on the air." Then the lover gives of himself completely (gives, that is, his "cap and bells"), and for the first time he draws a positive response from the beloved: "She opened her door and her window, / And the heart and the soul came through." Because of his absolute surrender of body and soul the beloved can finally welcome her lover.

The experience of the suitor described in "The Cap and Bells" seems to parallel the initiation of the romantic courtier into the sacred ritual of courtly love. The lady is elevated to a position of virtually divine respect, and the lover attempts to win her favor by a prescribed course of action: committing himself wholly to her will. The devotional benevolence of the suitor overcomes the coyness of the lady through his unhesitating divestment of self-interest.

The prosodic device of "The Cap and Bells" worth noticing in this respect is the cumulative use of language, a characteristic present in only one other of Yeats's lyrics ("Byzantium"). In "The Cap and Bells" there is a repetition of 75 percent of the words (excluding articles, prepositions, and pronominal forms), so that by the time we reach the last three stanzas we meet, in three-quarters of the lines, with only one new word per line (the remaining one-quarter having no more than two new words per line). As though to climax this kind of duplication the last line of the poem—"and the quiet of love in her feet"—contains no word that had not been used earlier. Once aware of the word repetition we have the feeling that there is an increasing melodic ease in the movement of the verse line.[4] And the range of meaning in the poem is restricted by the word repetition no more than a limited scale restricts the expression of any musical form. In the case of "The Cap and Bells" the total effect of the repetition is to establish for the poem a symbolically lyric environment—recreating that atmosphere in which the poem, according to Yeats, was originally conceived.

In no other lyric was Yeats able to give with such apparent ease so delicate a sense of harmony as he did in "The Cap and Bells." In this poem there is none of the psychological tension—the sense of foreboding, the aura of sorrow, the feeling of unfulfillment—that is written into his other early lyrics. The unconscious origin of this poem allowed the poet an ideal realm of beauty, an intense moment uncompromised by the awareness of any actual situation. The necessary separation between lover and beloved, a condition over which Yeats was to agonize for years, in "The Cap and Bells" is bridged by the extended magic of the poetic moment—all the speaker's irony, self-consciousness, and anxiety dissolved in the reality of the dream-vision. Heart and soul, garden and house, jester and queen are made to give way with melodic grace to a wishful marriage or transcendence of the separated images. What we become aware of at last in the poem is a supersensory stability of that marriage, captured as it is from the invisible fabric and perpetual flux of dreamed images.

Yeats's early poetry, as many critics have pointed out, is bathed in the twilight atmosphere of dream. That this represents quite an ephemeral state should not detract from the fact that it is nonetheless perfectly realized in "The Cap and Bells."

What though about the other love poems? It is evident that the love relationship depicted in those poems falls short of the ideal realized through dream. The memory of, or the unsatisfied longing for, the ideal haunts the speaker in these poems and, at best, can inform his appeal to love with gentle irony. More often, the lover's state of mind is felt by the reader to be disturbingly divided. The love vision takes the form of an apocalyptic vision; the everyday conflict of emotions and ideas is regarded only as an obstacle to union with the beloved, and for this reason the temporal world is wished away.

Yeats's unconscious attraction to the dream-ideal of love and beauty was reinforced by the image he cultivated of Maud Gonne. But all Maud could do was disappoint the poet with any manifestation of the ideal. "Always since I was a boy," Yeats recalled, "I have questioned dreams for her sake—and she herself always a dream and deceiving hope." [5] Maud herself had committed her life to an ideal, but it was grounded in a political faith that depended on "memorable action." [6] Before he really knew Maud, Yeats could say "I sympathise with her love of the national idea" (*KT,* 89, March 1889), and he came to see in her fiery and noble character the archetype of Ireland itself. This alone was enough to immortalize Maud in his eyes. But at the same time he could not help but be dismayed at her insistence on marrying "the national idea" to the revolutionist belief in violence.[7] She compromised her nobility, Yeats felt, because the principle of revolution was always in danger of being betrayed by people who were motivated by personal hatred or by the prospect of private gain.

It is from the debased ethic described in Part II of "The Two Trees" that Yeats wanted to protect Maud. He was conscious not only of his need for her, as someone in whom he could vest his ideal, but also of "her need for protection and peace." [8] That meant wresting the virgin warrior from the crowd, and attempting to impose on her his own introspective personality ("Beloved, gaze in thine own heart," as the speaker says admonishingly in "The Two Trees"). What this would do was make Maud insist all the more on a life of action. "I have no time to think of myself," she claims to have told Yeats.[9] An ironic kind of selflessness: it left the poet alone with his vision, having always to compromise his devotional ideal (cf. "The Countess Cathleen in Paradise") with solitude, or with condescension to the beloved (cf. "The Pity of Love")—an ambivalence that persisted as long as he wrote poetry with the image of Maud in mind. ("She is my innocence and I her wisdom" is the way Yeats explained his two-sided relationship.) [10]

Under conditions such as these the frustrated lover would be inclined to cultivate his apocalyptic love vision. Possessed by his ideal image of the beloved, he can express only feelings of despair. It may be he can find in his own distraction reason for sympathetic repercussions in the universe at large (see "Maid Quiet"). Or he may entertain a wistful longing for the end of the world ("He wishes his Beloved were Dead"). Or again, his longing may be commensurate with his need to protect the loved one from the disquieting powers of this world ("The Poet pleads with the Elemental Powers"). At times the lover may seem self-assured ("He tells of the Perfect Beauty"), and at times fearful, of the purer life he assumes will begin with the end of time ("To his Heart, bidding it have no Fear"). On still other occasions his unanswered need for love may call forth a vengeful cry for cosmic upheaval ("He mourns for the Change that came upon him and his Beloved, and longs for the End of the World"; "The Valley of the Black Pig").

The apocalyptic love poems written before 1897, in effect, witness the miscarriage of the lover's yearning for an other-worldly ideal. And because the speaker's orientation is toward an object or person external to himself, there can be, at last, the confession only of a feeling of unfulfill-ment. In these poems we find little of that purifying discouragement which, in certain of the middle and late poems is evidenced by the re-deeming—resounding—expression of "tragic joy."

For Yeats there could be no overriding joy without initial acceptance of personal defeat. It was not the world, in which the lover found him-self, that had to be destroyed, but the lover's desire for absolute fulfill-ment. There would be no joy so long as the suitor denied his own self-sufficiency—trusted to an ideal separate from his own being, and apart from the human condition.

To Yeats, Maud Gonne was the living image of an ideal, supersen-sual beauty; and she could serve but to cast a shadow on things of this world. In Olivia Shakespear, Yeats found a counter-image to Maud Gonne. "She seemed a part of myself," [11] Yeats said of Olivia: and not, like Maud Gonne, his anti-self. Whereas Maud had a vibrant personal-ity, Olivia was quiet, introspective. Like Yeats she was an artist, whose writing, the poet felt, had a "tremulous delicacy . . . a kind of fragile beauty" (*L,* 257). As a woman she was more approachable than Maud, her presence more reassuring. In contrast to the paradoxical charm of Maud, whose spiritual beauty was coupled with a life of action, Olivia seemed to him humanly compatible: endowed with a "beauty, dark and still," capable of sharing with him (as it proved, throughout most of their lives) the most intimate feelings.

What seemed most significant was the quality of Olivia's sensibility. Unlike Maud Gonne, who was puzzled by Yeats's insistence on defeat as a test of the intrinsic worth of a thing (*YM,* 154), Olivia represented to Yeats the inimitable attraction of "defeated things." [12] What struck him the first time he saw her was her "sensitive look of destruction"— "an incomparable distinction," he felt. Unlike Maud's, Olivia's nobility was undemonstrative. She was self-possessed without being conspicuous; heroic without being assertive. At the time of her death, in 1938, Yeats eulogized her in recalling that "she came of a long line of soldiers and during the last war thought it her duty to stay in London through all the air raids" (*L,* 916). As for her beauty, Yeats went on, that was but one aspect of her most attractive attribute: her sense of "solitude." "No matter what happened she never lost her solitude" (*L,* 916). That was the heroic quality Yeats admired in her; she was able to withstand the impress of time and circumstance—and with remarkable reserve was able to brave even the prospect of personal loneliness.

The ineradicable impression left on Yeats by Maud Gonne did not, finally, allow room for his "new love." From the start, his affair with Olivia Shakespear seemed to Yeats only an interlude: "after all, if I could not get the woman I loved it would be a comfort, even but for a little while, to devote myself to another." The image he had of Maud Gonne was too sacred, her beauty too "incompatible with private intimate life." It was for this reason that he tended to regard his physical attraction to Olivia as the betrayal of a higher love. "No doubt my excited senses had their share in this argument [his decision to devote himself to Olivia] but it was an unconscious one." Whatever comfort his sexual involvement brought, it could never be complete. The "perpetual virginity of the soul," as he called it—the cause and consequence of his spiritual marriage with Maud (imperfectly consummated in 1898 and again in 1908) [13]—could only stand in the way of any continued intimacy with Olivia. And Olivia no doubt knew him too well to suppose her love for him could ever be fully reciprocated. "That is a poor way of loving," she reflected in one of her novels: "You fall in love with a girl's beautiful face—it's not the first time you've done it; you endow her with all sorts of qualities; you make her into an idol; and the whole thing only means that your aesthetic sense is gratified." [14]

And it is with precisely this—the effect Yeats's affair with Olivia Shakespear had on his "esthetic sense"—that we are principally concerned. One certainly cannot discount the fact that at some time during the interlude with Olivia (lasting from the spring of 1894 to the fall of 1895) Yeats wrote to her "several poems all curiously alike in style"; and, either because of this or as a result of this, he "thought I was once more in love." [15]

"The Shadowy Horses" was one of these poems, according to Yeats's own testimony; undoubtedly another was "The Travail of Passion," originally published as a companion poem to "The Shadowy Horses" (January 1896); and, I propose, he was referring also to two other poems, "The Heart of the Woman" (first published in July 1894) [16] and "The Lover asks Forgiveness because of his Many Moods" (published in November 1895). Eight other poems, not addressed to Olivia Shakespear but probably written with her image in mind, were "He remembers Forgotten Beauty," "A Poet to his Beloved," "He gives his Beloved certain Rhymes," "He Tells of a Valley full of Lovers," "He reproves the Curlew," "The Lover mourns for the Loss of Love," "He hears the Cry of the Sedge," and "He thinks of his Past Greatness when a Part of the Constellations of Heaven." [17]

What distinguishes these from other of Yeats's love poems is their use of sensuous images, the first to appear in his poetry. They are primarily the images of falling hair, dimmed or dream-heavy eyes, lingering hands and pale breasts. In all but one of the poems ("The Lover mourns for the Loss of Love"), the speaker pictures the lover embracing the beloved, or the beloved poised above, comforting the lover. The love-pose is typical of pre-Raphaelite poetry, but what is peculiarly Yeatsian about it is that it is usually charged with emotional ambivalence.

Unlike the edenic certainty of "The Cap and Bells," a troubled feeling pervades Yeats's sensuous love poems. The repeated allusions to sorrow, paleness, dimness help create a foreboding, twilight atmosphere. The musical, hypnotic rhythms of certain lines are offset by other rhythms that are more rhythmical or free-flowing. The sensuous images contrast with images of a higher love, or images of destruction and isolation. The compatibility of the lovers is felt to reflect an unsettling, passing mood. Although Yeats uses images quite similar to those used by Rossetti in *The House of Life* (a fact often pointed out), the mood of Yeats's poems is strikingly different: there is nothing in his use of images which suggests the ultimate harmony of physical and spiritual awareness, characteristic of Rossetti's love poetry.[18]

The earliest of Yeats's sensuous love poems is "The Heart of the Woman." It is one of two early poems (the other being "The Song of the Old Mother") told from a woman's point of view. It is not typical of any other love poem, early or late, in that the confidence of the speaker seems almost completely to override any suggestion of spiritual conflict. The comforts of home and prayer are put aside, the speaker would have us believe, because the call of love is so urgent and self-absorbing. Even the threat of the storm outside is kept beyond reach of the lovers.

> . . . The shadowy blossom of my hair
> Will hide us from the bitter storm.

> O hiding hair and dewy eyes,
> I am no more with life and death,
> My heart upon his warm heart lies,
> My heart is mixed into his breath.

This ending would provide a nice contrast with the dream ending of "The Cap and Bells," were it not that the idealized conclusion seems somewhat forced. Can the physical relationship be so easily resolved, we wonder. Not unless we grant that the speaker is utterly caught up in the wings of her own emotion, for a moment disallowing the intruding influence of warm memories and "bitter storm." If we compare it with the other love poems, "The Heart of the Woman" seems an anomaly. The optimism of the speaker is too insistent not to be, finally, problematical.

In "The Travail of Passion," a poem published a year and a half after "The Heart of the Woman," the situation is more understandably complex. The speaker in lines 1 through 5 could, at first, be taken to be an undifferentiated "we": the lover and beloved as one. But then as we read the final three lines—

> [6] We will bend down and loosen our hair over you,
> [7] That it may drop faint perfume, and be heavy with dew,
> [8] Lilies of death-pale hope, roses of passionate dream

—we become suddenly aware that it is the woman now who must be speaking. At first (ll. 1 through 5) the lover and the beloved seem to find comfort in that they share a mysterious pain—"Our hearts endure the scourge, the plaited thorns, the way / Crowded with bitter faces, the wounds in palm and side, / The vinegar-heavy sponge, the flowers by Kedron stream." The physical passion of love is threatened by another, "immortal," passion; and the resulting conflict reminds the speaker of the ordeal at Calvary. The unitive point of view, whether suggested or intended, collapses at line 6.[19] What we are aware of finally is that the woman is trying to reassure the lover against a growing uneasiness. The pull on the lover's spiritual consciousness presumably will weaken his physical attraction to the mortal beloved. By dropping her hair over him the beloved hopes to quiet the lover's "immortal passion." But the speaker's tone cannot seem anything but disquieting. The long undulating lines carry with them an ironic music. The comforting voice of the speaker tries to embrace the contrary feelings of the lover, by this means attempting to dilute his obsessive vision of "the flaming lute-thronged angelic door" (line 1). We are left with the impression that it is only an apparent resolution that concludes the poem; the speaker's words can no more than suspend our awareness of the spiritual-physical tension underlying the momentary calm.

In "The Lover asks Forgiveness because of his Many Moods," the anxiety of the speaker, the man, dominates. The image of the ideal reality—of faery or of the Blessed Isles of Celtic lore—overshadows the immediate presence of the beloved. The distraught lover bids the beloved recall to him the memory of those aspiring to the world of immortals, as though that might ease the pain of his separation from the beloved. Perhaps her mournful incantation will wipe out the memory it invokes; perhaps the lover will become reconciled to his perpetual disquiet. The ending is ambiguous, though more suggestive of the lover's resignation to an other-worldly ideal than of a continuing intimacy between him and his mistress.

> . . . Cover the pale blossoms of your breast
> With your dim heavy hair,
> And trouble with a sigh for all things longing for rest
> The odorous twilight there.

The ending of "He bids his Beloved be at Peace" is also ambiguous, but in this poem the balance is redressed in favor of the temporal reality. The twilight world of "Sleep, Hope, Dream, endless Desire" seems about to give way to the apocalyptic vision; but the "tumultuous song" that accompanies the realization of that vision (viz., "The Lover asks Forgiveness . . . ," l. 20) is heard with ominous overtones.

> I hear the Shadowy Horses, their long manes a-shake,
> Their hoofs heavy with tumult, their eyes glimmering white.

The lover turns his back on the four horses announcing physical devolution, himself believing his mortal love can hold out against their inevitable approach.

> The Horses of Disaster plunge in the heavy clay:
> Beloved, let your eyes half close, and your heart beat
> Over my heart, and your hair fall over my breast,
> Drowning love's lonely hour in deep twilight of rest,
> And hiding their tossing manes and their tumultuous feet.

The comfort of physical love, and the desire to be rid of immortal longing, makes the lover want this world. But how long he can stave off the impending dawn—the intrusion of a supernatural light—is a matter left unanswered, in spite of the seeming resolution of the last four lines.

Like the "rough beast" in "The Second Coming" the "Shadowy Horses" is a transformation symbol, but the speaker's evocation of the image of the horses is not as effective as the speaker's summoning of the animal image in the later poem: the lover's attention is divided, and without the psychological depth of the mystery envisioned in "The Second Coming." The horses, as an image recalled from Celtic myth (*P,* 808), along with the image of the beloved, impinge on the consciousness of the speaker, but they do not emerge from any inherent, organically conceived, archetypal matrix. Compared with the "rough beast" both images in "He bids his Beloved be at Peace" share a relatively external frame of reference. And what is especially significant in the poem is that the images are put into a precarious balance with each other: so that the sensuous imagination tempers the immediacy of the apocalyptic vision.

The tentative equilibrium, however, finally serves to make more evident the isolation of the lover. That the latter should have to ask the beloved to drown with her presence "love's lonely hour" is an ironic request—suggesting not only the lover's quiet anxiety about the impending "disaster" but also his sense of being separate from, despite the closeness of, the beloved.

In three poems, two written probably before, and one written probably after "The Travail of Passion" and "He bids his Beloved be at Peace," the suggestion of spiritual pain or apocalyptic disaster is either absent or significantly weakened; and this is because the speaker is able to transpose the temporal into an eternal aspect of love.

In "He remembers Forgotten Beauty" (published July 1896) the speaker partakes of the best of two possible worlds, adroitly revealing an anagogical relationship between his mortal and immortal beloved, the physical and the supersensual beauty:

> [15] For that pale breast and lingering hand
> [16] Come from a more dream-heavy land,

> [17] A more dream-heavy hour than this;
> [18] And when you sigh from kiss to kiss
> [19] I hear white Beauty sighing too. . . .

We are not reminded of the "white eyes" of the "Shadowy Horses," or of the passion at Calvary. The transformation symbol is the person of the beloved—her physical manifestation:

> [1] When my arms wrap you round I press
> [2] My heart upon the loveliness
> [3] That has long faded from the world. . . .

The transformation is accompanied by a softening of the apocalyptic vision; all anxiety and sense of separation are resolved into an awesome regard for the ethereal realm: where "white Beauty" sighs and "her high lonely mysteries" oversee the quickening transparency of the temporal scene.

In "A Poet to his Beloved" the "white woman" is addressed directly —the "white woman that passion has worn." The contrary images of the beloved here are fused in the speaker's mind, with the passionate, temporal love in the process of giving way to the vision of love beyond "the pale fire of time." The same is true of "He gives his Beloved certain Rhymes": the lover bids the beloved bind up her long hair and put off the sensuous charms that gave him comfort, to become her transcendent, saint-like self who sighs for all men, and for whom "all men's hearts must burn and beat." The lover's magnanimity thus heightens the personal relationship, and the figure of the mortal beloved thus seems of a kind with Yeats's old supernal image of the compassionate rose (cf. "The Rose of the World").

The supersensual music of "The Cap and Bells" is thus replicated in the devotional tone of these three love poems. Unlike the ambivalent attitude of the speaker in "He asks Forgiveness . . . ," "The Travail of Passion," and "He bids his Beloved be at Peace," the attitude of the speaker in the devotional lyrics is effected by transposition of the image of the mortal beloved. The irresistible beauty of the heavenly queen of "The Cap and Bells"—"her hair . . . a folded flower / . . . the quiet of love in her feet"—would seem to have redirected, and possibly transformed, the temporal attributes of a consoling, sensuous beauty: the heavy, dream-laden eyes, the lingering hands, pale breasts, and long brimming hair. If anything, the mortal beloved has served as a catalytic reinforcement, an intermediary between the lover's physical desire and his ultimate dream of a spiritual Quiet.

What the speaker has attempted to do in these love lyrics is "discover immortal moods in mortal desires, . . . a divine love in sexual passion" (*E*, 195). In effect, it is a significant step in the poet's attempt to find a suitable ground for symbolic meaning. But how long would the beloved allow herself to be used so? The sobering aftermath of the lover's relationship with the beloved is told in five poems that were written between 1896 and 1898: "He reproves the Curlew" (published November 1896), "He tells of a Valley full of Lovers" (published January 1897), "The Lover mourns for the Loss of Love," "He hears the Cry of the Sedge" (both published May 1898), and "He thinks of his Past Greatness when a Part of the Constellations of Heaven" (published October 1898).

A new note is sounded in these poems. For the first time in Yeats's poetry we hear the speaker's anguish. The lover is caught by his own devices. In the name of a higher love he has forfeited his mortal beloved, and whatever attempt he makes to assimilate the latter's sensuous qualities to his image of divine beauty serves merely to bring home to him the unattainability of his ideal. As a result neither the physical desire nor the spiritual aspiration is finally fulfilled. The lover has overreached himself and now can bear witness only to his own loneliness.

"He reproves the Curlew" is the first instance we have of the speaker's sense of physical isolation.

> O curlew, cry no more in the air,
> Or only to the water in the West;
> Because your crying brings to my mind
> Passion-dimmed eyes and long heavy hair
> That was shaken out over my breast:
> There is enough evil in the crying of wind.

The image of the beloved is but a memory, and the more devastating for that reason: her sensuous imprint upon the lover's imagination leaves him with a heightened sense of the emptiness around him. The poem is unique among Yeats's early love poems in that the physical landscape is brought sharply into the foreground, to emphasize the initiation of the lover into a new and gnawing awareness of the real world.

The physical setting is made to seem even more immediate in "He hears the Cry of the Sedge."

> I wander by the edge
> Of this desolate lake
> Where wind cries in the sedge:
> *Until the axle break*
> *That keeps the stars in their round,*
> *And hands hurl in the deep*
> *The banners of East and West,*
> *And the girdle of light is unbound,*
> *Your breast will not lie by the breast*
> *Of your beloved in sleep.*

This time it is the immortal beloved that dominates the imagination, but her reality is deeply colored by the image of physical love. And the beloved might as well be a memory, too, because she is held to be unattainable until the afterlife. Nonetheless, her mortal attributes come to haunt the lover; and confronted with the temporal reality, the lover's satisfaction wishing for the end of the world seems to be ambivalent. The wish for heavenly repose expressed in the last lines turns ironic when read also as the lover's immediate—physical—longing to "lie by the breast" of his beloved.

Lines one to three of this poem are especially striking because they describe a natural—and perhaps for the first time a realistic—setting. We are helped to a reading of these lines by this often quoted passage of Yeats concerning his double frustration: "It was a time of great personal strain and sorrow—since my mistress had left me no other woman had come into my life and for nearly seven years [1895–1902] none did. I was tortured with sexual desire and disappointed love. Often as I walked in the woods at Coole it would have been a relief to have screamed aloud." [20] Yeats made the first of his repeated visits to Coole in the late summer of 1896, and it may well be that his walks along the lake there suggested the setting for "He hears the Cry of the Sedge."

In "He thinks of his Past Greatness . . ." we have instead of a realistic setting a mythological one. The frustration of the speaker, however, is still felt; and the apocalyptic vision is informed with an even more sensuous—almost sensual—longing than is apparent in "He hears the Cry of the Sedge."

> I have drunk from the Country of the Young
> And weep because I know all things now. . . .
> . . . .
> I became a man, a hater of the wind,

Knowing one, out of all things, alone, that his head
May not lie on the breast nor his lips on the hair
Of the woman that he loves, until he dies.
O beast of the wilderness, bird of the air,
Must I endure your amorous cries?

Though the physical longing does not replace, it does transform the apocalyptic vision, calling into question the spiritual ascendancy of the immortal beloved.

In "He tells of a Valley full of Lovers" and "The Lover mourns for the Loss of Love" the mortal beloved is finally seen in contraposition to the ideal. And the lover has no hope of reconciling the differences between the two. In his mind the images of the women he loves are disjoined, and the kinds of love they represent become equally inaccessible. He is reduced to mourning the loss of his mistress, without being the least assured of the ideal beauty that has caused his separation from a "beautiful friend."

The Wind Among the Reeds leaves the speaker confronted with his own spiritual solitude. The hero, if we may anticipate the course of Yeats's middle and later poetry, can no longer appeal to the ideal of love, or the sexual experience, without finally consulting the direction of his personal Daimon. The image of the immortal beloved (in *Responsibilities*) comes to represent an heroic ideal, and the image of the mortally compatible Sheba serves the lover subsequently only as an indication of his own daimonic growth. In order to attain to the purification his being demands, the lover has to get rid of every unpurged image, disestablish the preconception of an external ideal, and discover beyond the abstract demands of the soul or the assertive demands of the body a transpersonal integrity. The visionary has to descend his ladder; the body has to be stripped bare. Unassimilated forms, abstracted from the poet's awareness of the real world, must be reassembled into a more flexible, more toughminded kind of vision. The visionary scene, with all its bewitching images, remains to be reabsorbed by a new grounding of the imagination. Only after reintegrating such images can the dreaming heart discover itself. And that is the lonely but ennobling prospect open to the abandoned lover of *The Wind Among the Reeds*.

the solitary man:
emergence of the daimonic image
in the later love poems

No love poem Yeats wrote was so perfectly conceived, or self-contained, as "The Cap and Bells." But the kind of love envisioned in that poem precluded any sense of mortal compatibility. Everything that in his waking life fell short of the ideal would prove to the dreamer cause for discontent, anxiety, even hatred. The mortal condition could seem only like expulsion from Eden, without anything to compensate for the sense of loss.

Not until the loss is accepted will the lover be likely to overcome his dependence, his desire, his wish to possess or be possessed by what he loves. In order not to surrender his soul in the name of some power greater than his own (as he said George Russell felt himself in danger of doing [*L,* 838]), the poet had to discover the source of that power in spiritual solitude. Like the old "man I praise . . . in Tara's Halls," he whose objective is personal integrity would ask nothing of life: " 'God I have loved, but should I ask return / Of God or woman, the time were come to die' " (*P,* 609). Nothing but passionate disengagement, Yeats believed, will satisfy both "soul and self," and make the in-felt, progressive, release of emotion—not desire, longing, or self-assertiveness—the essential expression of human experience.

This attitude entailed a gradual change in emphasis in Yeats's love poetry from about 1898 onward. As a result of disillusionment the lover reverts from an outer to an inner-directed ideal. Love, as a spiritual ultimate, becomes incorporated into the lover's intrinsic awareness of a transpersonal Self, and this in turn spawns his need for a complementary, secular love—the marital relation and sexuality.

Study of the later love poetry can be begun by considering what is generally taken to be the first of Yeats's modern poems, "Adam's Curse." It is a poem that emerges from a seasoned sense of disillusionment. We feel in the speaker's expression of resignation the separation between lover and beloved. The "old high way of love" has taken its toll, the narrator tells us. And for the first time—the academic situation of the early poem "Ephemera" aside—the lover can accept his loneliness without crying out. This is because the lover as speaker seems to have been able to look in on himself, and to find the means now to disengage his feelings of sorrow, and remorse.

The parting of lovers is bittersweet because the lover takes the situation in hand. Earlier it was the incomparable beauty of the beloved that moved the speaker; now the cult of beauty has worn through its outward mystery. What remains for him is a sad but tender feeling of disenchantment; and we are aware that the lover has become the artist, outspoken and yet reserved in his judgment.

The poem is the beautiful thing now, and the poet's craft finds its place in the speaker's scale of values. The work of art is no longer a humble offering to the immaculate conception of beauty, as are the earlier love poems which focus on the image of Maud Gonne (see "A Poet to his Beloved").

What "Adam's Curse" does is capture a mood, and this is felt in the subject as well as in the effect of the poem. The writing of poetry, as a topic for discourse and as an actual experience, acts as a buffer for the disillusionment the speaker feels about the beloved. The talk about poetry, addressed apparently to both women in the company of the speaker, and the frank but formal exchange about "love" and "beauty" that ensues, between "that beautiful, mild woman, your close friend . . . and I," is a kind of parlor prelude to the speaker's more intimate, "unspoken," thoughts; these the lover, *l'amant passé,* would confide to the silent member of the trio (the "you" to whom "Adam's Curse" is addressed) through the open privacy of the poem.

Never before in Yeats have we been made so aware of the dramatic setting as a psychological component of the poem, evoking mood as a bridge between the inner and the outer reality.[1] With the brilliant stroke of a single opening line the scene is set: "We sat together at one summer's end. . . ." A Chekhovian melancholy, the sense of lingering regret, is suggested by the barest reference to time and place. Then, with a recapitulation of setting in the second last stanza the speaker is brought closer to the boundary between the real world and the realm of imagination:

> We sat grown quiet at the name of love;
> We saw the last embers of daylight die,
> And in the trembling blue-green of the sky
> A moon, worn as if it had been a shell
> Washed by time's waters as they rose and fell
> About the stars and broke in days and years.

This is no ordinary moon: it is seen in the mind's eye as well as in nature. It is a composite image (hinging on the associations of the word "shell") summing up the lover's now weary anticipation of time's end. The startling eschatology of the early love poems has greatly weakened, and the speaker turns to the moon as to an image that will convey his sense of personal enervation. It is a correlative suggesting the waning of the old, external ideal of beauty, and the gradual ebbing of the pitched emotion which makes the lover impatiently wish away the temporal world.

The moon image deserves singling out. It is one of those terminal images in Yeat's poetry which grow quite naturally out of the situation—the physical and the emotional setting—of the poem, and which attempt to embody the progression of ideas that constitutes the poem (cf. "Among School Children," "The Second Coming," "Byzantium," "The Statues"). The "moon" in "Adam's Curse" is a foreboding image of time and concludes with a mournful irony the talk about love and beauty. In a sense it foreshadows the use of the "moon" (ca. 1915) as a central symbol, "the great wheel," of the visionary "system" by which Yeats traces the evolution of the Self.

What Yeats needed most was something to sever the cord, shock him out of his hopeless attachment to Maud Gonne. It is ironic that not many months after the writing of "Adam's Curse" Maud was married. That poem, as Hone points out, is the refashioning of an event that actually took place between Yeats, Maud, and her sister Kathleen;[2] but except for the first stanza, the speaker meets the situation with the "gentle, sensitive mind" that the poet later complains is the debilitating mode of modern poetry (*P, 368*). The speaker, to be sure, admirably reflects the image of the thoughtful lover (who finds comfort in the surprising but delicate revelation of his ennui); he is not yet, however, the tough-minded counter-image of himself who with cavalier resolve outrides his disillusionment. It is the seeking of that image not himself, nor that of his beloved, that must serve in the end to rehabilitate the "sensitive mind," and at the same time radically transform the old haunting image of vestal beauty.

In *The Shadowy Waters* Yeats suggests the necessary change. The poem-play, as T. S. Eliot observed, seems "one of the most perfect expressions" of a pre-Raphaelite beauty.[3] But it is different from any of the love poetry Yeats had written until then in that the roles of the principals are reversed. Both lover and beloved appear to be moving, in a dialogical relationship, toward an awareness which conditionally embraces the real world; the beloved comes under the spell of the lover, plighting herself to the latter in a search for what proves to be their mutual acceptance of human solitude.

The direction of *The Shadowy Waters* is toward the working out of a spiritual compatibility in terms of the human condition. Yeats was highly concerned as to what he meant to say in this play,[4] and as a result was preoccupied with it longer than he was with any other piece of his: from as early perhaps as 1884 until 1906.[5] In this span of time Yeats had his liaison with Olivia Shakespear and his spiritual marriage with Maud Gonne; and it is probable that both women had their influence on the evolving relationship between Dectora and Forgael.[6]

S. B. Bushrui suggests that the more stringent language of the 1903–1904 rewriting of the play reflects the effect Maud's marriage to John MacBride had on Yeats. And to be sure the play offers an imaginative (and strangely prophetic) solution to a comparable situation: the husband-king stands in the way of the predestined lovers, and is put to death. But the dramatic situation actually long anteceded Maud's relationship with John MacBride. (We may suggest in passing that since Yeats was hard at work rewriting the play at the time he was becoming intimate with Mrs. Shakespear [*L*, 236, 1894], it is more probable that Dectora's mismarriage first became meaningful to Yeats in terms of the difficulties between Olivia and her husband.[7])

But no biographical speculations will really satisfy the imaginative content of the play. It is best here to turn to the climax of the dialogue between Forgael and Dectora and to see how their particular conflict is resolved.

Forgael, we are led to believe, has been searching all his life for what Dectora comes to represent to him, but once he has found Dectora and won her he begins to doubt his own intentions. He declares that he has "deceived" the woman, because he can share with her only his solitude: he is searching for love, "but of a beautiful, unheard-of kind / That is not in the world" (*P,* 228). For her part, Dectora proves to be only accidentally in love with her husband (who has been murdered by Forgael's crew). Gradually she yields to Forgael: through him she is spellbound into an awareness of the Blessed Isles "where the children of Aengus wind / In happy dances under a windy moon." In effect, she has assumed for herself Forgael's dream:

> What do I care
> Now that my body has begun to dream,
> And you have grown to be a burning sod
> In the imagination and intellect? (*P,* 245)

Because she has too quickly taken over his dream Forgael feels he has deceived her:

> I weep because I've nothing for your eyes
> But desolate waters and a battered ship.
>
> . . . .
> I weep—I weep because bare night's above,
> And not a roof of ivory and gold. (*P,* 246)

The dream of the Blessed Isles, Forgael tells her, should not be confused with time or place. Dectora does not understand and longs to be with Forgael only in "some sure country, some familiar place" (*P,* 249). Then she asks, giving over the hope of any transcendent dream: "Have we not everything that life can give / In having one another" (*ibid.*). Forgael now cannot be dissuaded from what he begins to realize is a quest for spiritual identity: he is led by his Daimon, not by her beauty or her will to live. When Dectora declares:

> I will cover up your eyes and ears
> That you may never hear the cry of the birds,
> Or look upon them.

Forgael replies:

> Were they but lowlier
> I'd do your will, but they are too high—too high. (*P,* 250).

He argues that she too can discover reality, and become aware of her identity, since only after this is done, Forgael claims, can they become

true lovers. And he looks for his precedent to the immortal Aengus and
Edain ("the wandering lovers, / To whom all lovers pray" [*P*, 224])—

> Our love shall be like theirs
> When we have put their changeless image on. (*P*, 250)

Dectora will not wholly abandon life. But she will compromise.
When it comes to deciding between going to a "familiar" or to a "deso-
late" place, Dectora decides for the latter, because there at least she will
have Forgael. She says with joy:

> The world drifts away,
> And I am left alone with my beloved,
> Who cannot put me from his sight for ever.
> We are alone forever and I laugh,
> Forgael, because you cannot put me from you. (*P*, 251)

The play proposes an ideal solution to the spiritual search in that Forgael
and Dectora, together, come to share a comparable awareness of solitude. Because of Dectora's surrender, Forgael is able to lower his sights,
and discover in himself the mystery of his quest. The play ends with
Forgael's declaring that their solitude (rather than passing through actual death) is what makes them "immortal" and that their growing immortal depends on the realization of a mythic reality which can "live in
us":

> Beloved, having dragged the net about us,
> And knitted mesh to mesh, we grow immortal;
> And that old harp awakens of itself
> To cry aloud to the grey birds and dreams,
> That have had dreams for father [Aengus? The Blessed Dead?
>   The Daimon?] live in us. (*P*, 252)

Although Yeats claimed that "the logic and circumstances" of *The
Shadowy Waters* "are all wrong," he felt the play is "right in its highest
moments" (*L*, 454, July 1905). And as with "The Cap and Bells," this
meant that the subject of the work was purposely ambiguous. However
the play once read, now in 1905 it allowed Yeats to ground his speculations about life and death. The famous program note for the perfor-
mance of the play on July 9, 1905 tries to steer the reader through possibilities of meaning to what was at the time the poet's own metaphysical

conclusion. Contrasted with "The Cap and Bells," *The Shadowy Waters* (if we follow the note) has a more human perspective—arguing for an exchange between man and woman in which there is a spiritual incarnation of the "living will."

> The main story expresses the desire for a perfect and eternal union that comes to all lovers, the desire of Love to 'drown in its own shadow.' But it has also other meanings. Forgael seeks death; Dectora has always sought life; and in some way the uniting of her vivid force with his abyss-seeking desire for the waters of Death makes a perfect humanity. Of course, in another sense, these two are simply man and woman, the reason and the will, as Swedenborg puts it.
>
> The second flaming up of the harp [*PL*, 109, a stage direction in the acting version, just before Forgael's concluding speech] may mean the coming of a more supernatural passion, when Dectora accepts the death-desiring destiny. Yet in one sense, and precisely because she accepts it, this destiny is not death; for she, the living will, accompanies Forgael, the mind, through the gates of the unknown world. Perhaps it is a mystical interpretation of the resurrection of the body.[8]

Ellmann is probably quite justified in linking *The Shadowy Waters* to Yeats's preoccupation in the late nineties with evolving a mystery rite to replace outworn religion.[9] In looking back on those years Yeats recognized the key role the idealized woman necessarily played in that rite, the mystery, no doubt, having derived from Yeats's personal experience of love. That "life is ritual," he said recalling Lionel Johnson's pronouncement, "expressed something that was in some degree in all our thoughts." "And how could life be ritual," he observed not without irony, "if woman had not her symbolic place?" (*A*, 201)

The Shadowy Waters reflects the occult influences of Yeats's early period, but it also has root in the middle period, when the ascendancy of the woman is counterbalanced by the influence of the Self-informed spirit Yeats called his spiritual Daimon. We may simply note here a matter that will be discussed in the succeeding chapter: in the volumes *The Green Helmet and Other Poems* and *Responsibilities* (1910) we find the symbolic woman no longer presides over the realm of ideal beauty, but has been transformed into the heroic ideal, a counterpart, if not prototype of the daimonic being the admirer himself aspires to become. But our concern at present is in following through the change in attitude of the lover, concentrating on how the speaker in the poem handles the renewed dichotomy—the persisting images of the mortal and the immortal beloved.

"The Collar-Bone of a Hare," dated July 5, 1915,[10] recalls the theme of the original plan for *The Shadowy Waters;*[6] instead of the twilight brooding of the poem-play, however, Yeats gives the tone of the lyric a jaunty twist. The lover has turned cavalier. Traveling alone, he would "cast a sail on the water / Where many a king has gone" and alight on what would seem to be an island with "comely trees and . . . lawn." He imagines himself a free man, able to join in "dancing" and / "learn that the best thing is / To change my loves while dancing." He will be gayly indifferent. Everything in his native land that may have caused dismay or hatred will have been rendered innocuous by the safe distancing of his imagination; he will stare through "the collar-bone of a hare / Worn thin by the lapping of water"; and instead of ending with a regretful sigh, as in "Adam's Curse," he will cut through his disillusionment with "tragic joy," exulting in the thought that he bears witness to, rather than shares in, the foibles of old acquaintances in an alien world:

> I would .   .   .   .
> .   .   .   .   stare
> At the old bitter world where they marry in churches,
> And laugh over the untroubled water
> At all who marry in churches,
> Through the white thin bone of a hare.

The "thin bone of a hare" circumscribes with irony the speaker's view of life. The speaker, though, does not escape the world: he inures himself to it by a resilient strategy of the imagination.[11]

It is difficult not to be reminded by the poem of Maud Gonne's marriage with John MacBride. Maud had converted, and was married in a Roman Catholic church.[12] But that was a full twelve years before, and these last ten years she was separated from her husband. This situation permitted Yeats to continue hoping she would reciprocate his love. After all, he still felt himself committed to the romantic vow he made as a young man: it may be, he conjectured, "I should never marry in church but I would love one woman all my life."[13] Two months after MacBride was executed for his part in the Easter Rebellion (1916) Yeats went to France and, by way of trying to "protect" Maud, again proposed to her; but he had strict reservations now, as though to prepare himself, and her, for her blank refusal. Then, the next year (August to September 1917) he found himself courting Maud's adopted daughter, as if intentionally to run the gamut of disappointment. The self-assured tone of

"The Collar-Bone of a Hare" in retrospect thus must have seemed to Yeats an ironic prelude to his own overtures of marriage in the two years that followed the writing of that poem.

On October 21, 1917 Yeats was married to Georgie Hyde-Lees (at the Harrow Road register office in London). There was no ardent courtship, their marriage having followed as it did upon refusals from Maud and Iseult. Yeats had known Miss Hyde-Lees more or less casually since 1911. She was related by marriage to Olivia Shakespear (through whom Yeats first came to know Georgie's family) and, like Olivia, she seemed to Yeats to be Maud's opposite. Yeats had fairly exhausted his pursuit of ideal beauty, and was relieved having finally committed himself to Miss Hyde-Lees rather than to Maud. He was averse to marrying Maud Gonne because of her single-minded involvement in politics (she could always be counted on to "do something wild" [*L*, 632]). In addition, her lifelong fascination with an ideal rendered distasteful any kind of feminine subservience, either in a marital or in a sexual relationship. Georgie, on the other hand, was amenable as a woman, had domestic virtues, was "kind, wise, unselfish," capable of making "my life serene and full of order." The marriage was a milestone in his life: "From being more miserable than I ever remember being since Maud Gonne's marriage I became extremely happy" (*L*, 633). He was referring at the time to the strain his relationship to Iseult had put on him, and to the cure his wife was effecting by revealing unexpectedly their psychical compatibility.

Richard Ellmann believes that Yeats's marriage initiated the period of his greatest poetry: had he not married or had he died instead of marrying in 1917 he would have been known only as a "remarkable minor poet." What Yeats's marriage did, we may say, was enable him to release untapped sources of energy, and to discover in the work of the imagination a spiritual pattern. According to Ellmann, the poet's new sense of security, serenity, and order derived from a "strength [which] enabled him to write lyric after lyric in which he spoke, with fresh confidence, in his own person." [14]

We must be careful, though, not to overread the consequences of Yeats's marriage. The tension and sense of conflict in the poetry is perhaps more acute after than before 1917. And the poetry and visionary philosophy that emerge after 1917 is prepared for by the poet's state of mind *before* he decided to marry Georgie. The sessions with his wife that accounted for the writing of *A Vision* were indeed anticipated by Yeats's essay "Anima Hominis," completed in February 1917 when the poet was preoccupied by his relationship with Maud and Iseult. It is better to say that the external events of 1916–1917 propitiously paralleled Yeats's spiritual development and triggered off the critical issue which brought the poet, in the last throes of an idealistic love, face to face with himself and his own destiny. His break with Iseult and Maud and his acceptance of, and by, Georgie would seem to be the resolving point of that crisis he describes in *A Vision*—the point at which willful striving becomes indistinguishable from passive involvement in life—when chance and fate coincide: and there is no longer the agony of searching the external world for the initiating image of his spiritual vision. The accidental, almost offhanded, relationship with Miss Hyde-Lees (that they *might* be married was put in the form of an ultimatum to Iseult) proved to be a fruitful union, because perhaps for the first time the poet did not idealize his love, did not expect of this woman anything more than the companionship of a wife.

The conflict from this point on in Yeats's life was more deeply internal, the problem of a man trying to come to terms with himself. And it was precisely this, "the quarrel with ourselves," Yeats maintained, that makes for poetry ("Anima Hominis," *M,* 331). In section VIII of "Anima Hominis" Yeats explains the connection between love and the realization of Self. The lover, to paraphrase the involuted argument, is the potential victim of his spiritual Daimon; and his beloved is the incipient force in that spiritual conflict, the bridge and source of communion between self and Self, his personal and transpersonal being.

> . . . As somebody says in *Wilhelm Meister,* accident is destiny; and I think it was Heraclitus who said: the Daimon is our destiny. When I think of life as a struggle with the Daimon who would ever set us to the hardest work among those [tasks] not impossible, I understand why there is a deep enmity between a man and his destiny, and why a man loves nothing but his destiny. . . . I am persuaded that the Daimon delivers and deceives us, and that he wove that netting from the stars and threw the net from his shoulder. Then my imagination runs from Daimon to sweetheart, and I divine an analogy that evades the intellect. I remember that Greek antiquity has bid us look for the principal stars, that govern enemy and sweetheart alike . . . and that it may be 'sexual love,' which is 'founded on spiritual hate,' is an image of the warfare of man and Daimon; and I even wonder if there may not be some secret communion, some whispering in the dark between Daimon and sweetheart.

Yeats's concern in the essay is with the evolution of Self, and in this passage he implies that love is what helps a man become his own spiritual opposite. Sexual love or personal attachment then is not an end in itself. What Yeats means when he says "that the Daimon delivers and deceives us" is explained in the companion essay, "Anima Mundi": the daimon is a man's image of what he would ultimately be if he fulfilled his destiny; but because he must meet with, or else succumb to, images not of his own making—alien forces in the memory, in the blood, or in contemporary life that were inherited or impressed on him—he may be easily sidetracked attempting to resolve his fate.

The marital love poems of Yeats's middle and late periods differ from the love poems of his early period in that the overall controlling image is the Self in the process of becoming, rather than an ideal love or beauty. And 1917, the year of Yeats's marriage, is the date which marks this reversal.

Before turning to the marital and sexual love poems we might look at the last poems Yeats wrote prior to his marriage, poems which mourned, or celebrated, the loss of his old ideal. Conveniently enough, Yeats published these poems, half a dozen of them, as a series in *The Little Review* for June 1917. We have already discussed "The Collar-Bone of a Hare," the first of the six in order of composition. The series as a whole is interesting to consider for the progress the speaker makes in each poem in disposing of the controlling image of hopeless love or unavailing beauty.

Each of the poems appearing in *The Little Review* for June 1917 have the dates of composition appended to them, as though they might indicate a progression in the attitude of the narrator.[15] The first and last poems of the series taken in chronological order show the speaker apart from, or independent of, the image he contemplates: but his laughing, self-assured tone in "The Collar-Bone of a Hare" (the first poem, July 1915) has given way in the final poem "The Wild Swans at Coole" (October 1916) to a graceful and slow-moving meditative verse which leaves the words tinged with the sense of loss. In "The Wild Swans" images and landscape enjoy their own reality, the remorse of the speaker notwithstanding. As might be expected, the speaker's response to the world outside has been sharpened at the expense of some beautiful memory of his. The subject and mood of the poem is most clearly akin to that of "Adam's Curse," but its delicate molding, in spite of the subtle opposition, of image and feeling makes "The Wild Swans" the more perfectly conceived poem—a most satisfying, though belated, conclusion to Yeats's twilight poetry.

The intermediate poems in *The Little Review* series show the speaker less certainly removed from the images he confronts. In passing from "The Collar-Bone of a Hare" to "A Deep-sworn Vow" (October 1915) we are reminded that the lover's freedom—the prospect of his changing loves while dancing—does not take into account the fact that his "only love" has been unrequited: the beloved has not kept faith, and this only makes the speaker more intensely aware of her image haunting him. In "Broken Dreams" (November 1915) he assures himself at first that his memories of an unfulfilled love will dissolve into splendid reality: "in the grave all, all, shall be renewed. / The certainty that I shall see that lady / Leaning or standing or walking / In the first loveliness of womanhood, / . . . / Has set me muttering like a fool." And yet the vision of that loveliness turns on itself, reveals in the end not an assurance of future bliss, but the crumbling substance of things past, "an image of air: / Vague memories, nothing but memories." In "Presences" (November 1915) the memories take the form of hallucination. The spectral images of three women he has loved impose upon the speaker. They are first described climbing "up my creaking stair," "laughing or timid or wild, / In rustle of lace or silken stuff." And then their forms seem curiously fixed, immobile, archetypal perhaps in their bearing on the person describing them:

> They stood in the door and stood between
> My great wood lectern and the fire
> Till I could hear their hearts beating:
> One is a harlot, and one a child
> That never looked upon a man with desire,
> And one, it may be, a queen.[16]

In the fourth poem, "Men Improve with the Years" (July 1916), as in a related poem, "The Living Beauty" (written in 1917 and also published in *The Little Review,* a year later), the lover tries to get free of at least one of those three spectral forms.[17] In both poems the speaker interjects an image that he hopes will displace the obsessive reality: a "beauty that is cast out of a mould / In bronze, or . . . dazzling marble," or else an image of himself, the lover, transformed, "a weatherworn, marble triton / Among the streams." But these attempts by the speaker—to contain, and therefore control, the objective reality, or alternately to oppose to that reality a subjective image larger than the self (a correlative for what Yeats later calls "marmorean stillness"): such attempts are fractured with resistance on the part of a lover whose desire has been left too long unsatisfied.

The series of poems appearing in *The Little Review* invariably focus on the problem of the lover's cumulative solitude. Only in "The Collar-Bone of a Hare," the earliest of the poems, does the speaker seem to surmount the situation in which he is involved. But even here, the joy expressed by him is satisfying not so much because of what the poem is able to include as because of what it excludes. Only total acceptance can effect a radical change in the person of the lover. And that is a prospect not yet in evidence. The speaker meanwhile has to try bringing about a more balanced tension, to give full play to the physical-spiritual antinomy. The lover's mortal desire and immortal longing have somehow to be equalized before he can live with if not rejoice in his loneliness.

In what we may call the marital-love poems, written between 1914 and 1924, the speaker redresses the balance that in *The Wind Among the Reeds* weighed in favor of the immortal beloved. In these poems the unconditional union of lover and mortal beloved is especially favored. The image of the old ideal is felt as a painful intrusion in such a relationship. At the same time, however, the ideal remains, and its influence can only be redirected, not eliminated. We may observe that soon it will prove to have changed the lover's image of himself to something more than the comfortable figure of a bedmate or domestic companion.

"Solomon to Sheba" describes the standard against which the other marital-love poems may be measured. This delightful dialogue between lovers circles-in its own world much as does the dream poem "The Cap and Bells"; but the lovers in the later poem luxuriate in their mortal compatibility, and this makes the poem the antithesis of "The Cap and Bells." "Solomon to Sheba" contrasts too with "Adam's Curse" in that lover and beloved make a private paradise of their contentment, regarding the world as little more than "a narrow pound."

But "Solomon to Sheba" is also limited by its subject. The subject is satisfying only to the degree that the reader is not bothered by what is left out in the poem. If we want a more comprehensive awareness on the part of the speaker, then the happiness of the two lovers must seem to us as partial as that of the liberated lover in "The Collar-Bone of a Hare."

Other of the marital-love poems reintroduce the problematic element. And this is apparent from the earliest of the Solomon-Sheba poems, written in 1914. In "On Woman" the speaker opposes the compatible figure of Sheba to the haunting image of the immortal beloved. The latter is his ultimate destiny, but she is regarded now, in the present life, as a "perverse creature of chance": the lover's recurrent memory of her drives a wedge into his happiness. The mood of the poem is bifurcated, but the speaker begins with and returns to a description of that uncomplicated relationship he would desire with a woman. "May God be praised," he says "for woman / That gives up all her mind," who surrenders for a man's sake her own personality, and clothes "as with her flesh and bone" his guiding will and thought.

This kind of counterimage, of a woman who would bring order and serenity into the lover's life, the poet must have been nurturing for some time. Jeffares tells us that in his diaries for 1909 to 1912, Yeats made reference to Solomon and Sheba as symbols of "perfect love." [18] Yeats did have a mistress from about 1909 to 1912, and it is quite possible that her actuality gave credence to the image of Sheba; but does this necessarily exclude the possibility that "Sheba" could have derived from an earlier relationship with Olivia Shakespear, or that "she" may have anticipated Yeats's later relationship with Miss Hyde-Lees? Perhaps "Sheba" is best viewed as a composite image, an imaginable counterpart, rather than a specific person, in a persisting antinomy.

In order to lead Solomon "a dance" Sheba is made to contend both with the immortal beloved and the spiritual Daimon. In "An Image from a Past Life" it is the immortal beloved that she tangles with, an unpurged memory, that lingers in her mind because she feels her lover beside her is preoccupied with the same image. Her lover admits that the influence of that early ideal has not been forgotten—perhaps never will be—but now, he assures her, it can be construed as a benevolent influence, an image to make him fonder of her, his present love (l. 35).

In "Solomon and the Witch" a witch, or spiritual daimon, at first disturbs and then reassures Sheba. The witch's voice—"not his [the lover's], not mine"—speaks through Sheba as through a medium, and elicits from Solomon the delphic wisdom that each of the lovers brings to the marriage bed "an imagined image . . . / And finds a real image there." The lovers are to be reconciled only when their being together dissolves all expectation, and when they will have accepted "Chance" (as they would their own deliberate "Choice") by being joined through marriage. But is absolute reconciliation possible? [19] The lover goes on to say that some ambivalent factor determines their fate: "an image [that] is too strong / Or maybe is not strong enough." (This cryptic insight might well refer to the opposing influence of 1) the external ideal, transcending love or beauty, and 2) the spiritual Daimon, who internalizes desire, making the assertive self increasingly more tolerant of its unwilled fate.) For her part, the mortal beloved becomes more eager to break down the lover's resistance, through physical union: "'The night has fallen,'" she cries, "' . . . / And the moon is wilder every minute. / O! Solomon! let us try again.'"

The moon, however, is not primarily a lover's moon, but a symbol of internal change. In "Towards Break of Day" we have described to us the frustration of lovers who share their dream. The speaker is obsessed again by a memory of his past: "a waterfall / Upon Ben Bulben side / That all my childhood counted dear." The stone or the water is not something man can touch again, and feel as he once did; the time is gone when he can hail the mystery of the external event. At the most the event becomes a "prospect in the mind." [20]

Preoccupation with the mysterious and the unknown in "Towards Break of Day" does not allow for the consoling beauty of an aubade. Whatever his image means, the lover discovers it has haunted the beloved too, in "bitter sleep." The beloved dreamt of "the marvellous stag of Arthur, / That lofty white stag" that "leap[s] / From mountain steep to steep." This is probably another unpurged image, what Yeats calls an "Over Shadower" (*P,* 822), or else its converse, the Self-born image of an internal life. However it is construed, the beloved has reason to view the "marvellous" form with bitterness: it can only separate her from what she loves most.

"The Gift of Harun Al-Raschid," published in 1924, seven years after Yeats's marriage, emphasizes the point we have been trying to make about the love poetry of Yeats's middle and late period. Kusta Ben Luka, the Solomon figure, and narrator, in this poem, has a spiritual conception of love: "I / Who have accepted the Byzantine faith / . . . Think when I choose a bride I choose for ever." He tells of the young girl who wanted to share his life, right the wrongs that informed "my past" and now "lived . . . at my side." This girl was convinced of her place in his life, feeling that "time's disfiguring touch / Gave but more reason for a woman's care." Whatever it was that troubled him fascinated her, even as she tried to cure him of its adverse affects.

> . . . was it love of me, or was it love
> Of the stark mystery that has dazed my sight,
> Perplexed her fantasy and planned her care?

He then tells how at night he listened to her strange wisdom, the voice of a "great Djinn" that spoke through her. This man thought himself wise, and protector of her innocence. Now the situation is reversed. Through *her* the mystery of his own being is revealed, the driving force that all these years haunted him in the search for truth.

> She seemed the learned man and I the child;
> Truths without father came, truths that no book
> Of all the uncounted books that I have read,
> Nor thought out of her mind or mine begot,
> Self-born, high-born, and solitary truths. . . .

And for all her wisdom the girl has retained her innocence.

> . . . she rose and swept the house
> In childish ignorance of all that passed.
> Even to-day, after some seven years
> When maybe thrice in every moon her mouth
> Murmured the wisdom of the desert Djinns. . . .

It is as though this unconscious understanding of hers, and the love of this man, older than she, who discovers wisdom through love might make for a complementary relationship. With the other each may eventually become his or her opposite, and by such means, through marriage, resolve the "antimony" (V, 52): then man and woman would be in communion with their separate identities, spiritually whole and yet forever joined. That presumably is what the speaker means when he imagines

> 'The best that life can give,
> Companionship in those mysterious things
> That make a man's soul or a woman's soul
> Itself and not some other soul.'

But so far the attachment is one-sided. And the lover is now concerned that the girl has not passed beyond her first innocence: what if she finds out he loves her not for herself, but for the voice of a God in her, which proves to be the daimonic echo of his own Self?

> Were she to lose her love, because she had lost
> Her confidence in mine, or even lose
> Her first simplicity, love, voice and all,
> All my fine feathers would be plucked away
> And I left shivering.

Final wisdom is not possible without love. But love is not complete without wisdom. The girl is mediator between the lover and the spiritual being he has yet to understand. And to be sure, her physical being is more real than any intellectual abstraction. "All dreams of the soul," we are told, "End in a beautiful man's or woman's body" (*P,* 374). Yet it is his own understanding that allows the lover a glimpse of the mystery. The beauty he had formerly pursued gives way. Having adopted an heroic pose he finds strength in loneliness—a companion in arms, as it were, inscrutable and yet intelligible to him. Paradoxically, he does not betray his secret, even though he declares: "now my mystery is out." Having said that, he concludes by differentiating between beauty, wisdom, and the revelation of "solitary truth."

> A woman's beauty is a storm-tossed banner;
> Under it wisdom stands, and I alone—
> Of all Arabia's lovers I alone—
> Nor dazzled by the embroidery, nor lost
> In the confusion of its night-dark folds,
> Can hear the armed man speak.

Of what use is mortal love and human beauty? They are regarded, like their idealized counterparts, as a means, not an end, of daimonic vision. Solitude and wisdom are the alembic from which the lover's Self, the spiritual substance, is distilled. And that is the mystery, the "armed man" whose untold words are heard only by a person in touch with the source of his own identity. Whatever trials love or the quest for beauty has made him submit to, the lover at last returns to himself, briefed by a knowledge that cannot, finally, be shared.

The "armed man" is one of several terminal figures in Yeats's poems whose appearance is prompted by the meditative intensity of the speaker. The mysterious figure first appears as the *doppelgänger* in the last lines of "Ego Dominus Tuus"; it takes on a more menacing aspect in "The Second Coming" and "The Magi"; and with Yeats's very last work, "The Black Tower," it becomes virtually an invisible presence in the poem. We may say that the progression of the culminating images in these lyrics (including the "armed man" of "Harun Al-Raschid") is emblematic of a deepening sense of solitude on the part of the speaker.

The greater the sense of solitude the more alluring the prospect of death and spiritual consummation; but also the more human the attachment between lover and beloved. "Beauty drop[s] out of the loneliness / Of body and soul" (*P*, 375). Nothing imposed from without can command the imagination. The ideal, the perfect form, is what the eye trained on some outlying mystery demands; but the mind's eye, on the other hand, takes for its model the transformed image of the self, leaving the bodily senses—though soon to be put off—in closer touch with the real world. Love, then, as the response to a living person, and not a figuration of the mind, is possible. And "as the new love grows the sense of beauty will fade" (*V*, 140).[21]

The lover would drop his unearthly desire, and become as a "wise king . . . seek[ing] a woman who looks the wise mother of children." Human involvement would relate him to all "social life," allow him to "love what disillusionment gave" (*V*, 146–47). Perhaps, even, as the saint-like George Russell (*AE*),[22] the lover who has become sage might have been humbled enough to regard "all souls of equal value: the queen . . . not more than an old apple woman" (*A*, 315).

Self-realization for Yeats implied absolute equanimity, a state of mind which at last absolves him of selfish attachment. With this for a final prospect the lover can insist on physical love as an indispensable catalyst. As he would have Crazy Jane say, "love is but a skein unwound / Between the dark and the dawn"—the beginning and the end of conscious life: for she knows that "A lonely ghost the ghost is / That to God shall come" (*P*, 511).

But just because it is a weeding ground for the soul the body is blessed. "Man, woman, child (a daughter or a son), / That's how all natural or supernatural stories run," says Ribh (*P*, 556). Any realization of the supernatural is congenital with life. The soul has to give up its virginal pride. For the proud abstainer, man or woman, sexual experience may prove a sanctum of humility: " 'strip the body bare,' " as the reluctant lady in "The Three Bushes" proposes, and find " 'maybe we are all the same' " (*P*, 570).

As a man already past middle age Yeats must have found in sex an antidote to the idealizing energy that sapped his youth. But the antidote was not a substitute for the conceptual ideal. Crucial to his development was Yeats's radical awareness of a force continuous with his own existence, a spiritual energy taking hold of and remolding him from within —always contrary to, but never separate from, his consciousness of the self.

"My poetry all comes from rage and lust," Yeats told Dorothy Wellesley after completing "The Three Bushes" (*L,* 871, December 1936). He was aware of having found an ultrapersonal freedom, a nonrestrictive, forthright manner becoming the character of passionate women or of "a wild and wicked old man." He must have startled Lady Dorothy by declaring how transparent his passion was, allowing him to "make a woman express herself as never before." "It was no man who looked at you," he wrote, "it was the woman in me. . . . I have looked out of her eyes. I have shared her desire" (*L,* 868). Given this view it would be a mistake to suppose that the sexual love poems demonstrated an unmediated concern with sex. It was the transformation of personal desire Yeats was ultimately interested in, "Myself" that I "must . . . remake" (as the old man in "An Acre of Grass" puts it). Bitterness and sensuality became for Yeats the prepossessing legacy of a life spent in search of reality—and it is that which he met head-on with unprecedented vigor in his later poems.

To confront the visible world meant for the poet finally bending himself to the task of dissolving rage and lust, and by re-creative vision preparing for "one last song, sweet and exultant." An "old man's frenzy" will perhaps then have served its purpose, proving an "old man's eagle mind" which eventually "pierce [s through] the clouds" of his own being.

The resiliency of the imagination is not the result of limited perspective. And it is with this in mind that we have traced the course of Yeats's love poetry. The lover's vision of becoming one with the beloved is nothing short of romantic irony, but it is an irony that brings the visionary to the threshold of his proper province. The disillusionment that comes of having staked his earthly desires upon an otherworldly love engenders in a man the opposite course of action, making the soul "the world's servant, and as it serves, / Choosing whatever task's most difficult / Among tasks not impossible." Once involved in the dialectic which gives direction to life, the "world's servant" can better understand his role; and he marks down the temporal progression of contrary types —"Reformer, merchant, statesman, learned man / Dutiful husband, honest wife"—as a continuous process in the evolution of the Self (*P*, 376). The process and not the absolute becomes the immediate concern of poet or lover, so that the passing world may show him, through the transiency of form and image, personality and daily life, human traces of the mysterious and ineradicable "signature of reality."

vision and "responsibility":
"the second coming" in relation to the
"helen" poems and the early poems of exultation

The heroic quest for Yeats was a perdurable subject for poetry, explored first in the longest and one of the earliest of his poems, *Oisin* (1889). Almost immediately after *Oisin,* love, the longing for everlasting union with the beloved, became the poet's principal concern; and after that Yeats dealt with the lover's anguish and disillusionment (1897–1905). This in turn became the basis for reaffirmation of an heroic discipline, evidenced in poems which made the immortal beloved an epical rather than an ethereal figure, the personification of a martyred ideal, noble and solitary in her ways (1908–1915). The lover's adoration of the beauty of the Rose of Ireland had given way to a worshipful respect for the fading beauty of a latter-day Helen, the "phoenix" whose country betrayed her romantic zeal and whose defeat seemed to her admirer only to increase her stature.

From about 1910 the speaker himself (with his "Helen" as an example) adopts the heroic pose, sounding the clarion call of "joy in defeat," learning to exult in spite of the seemingly insurmountable opposition of the petty and frenetic world around him. The magnetic core of Yeats's poetry deepens as the poet's horizons broaden. The social and political world is taken on as a challenge to the soul, and if conflict leads to defeat, that is what strikes the spark of enlightenment, the spiritual reserve that holds against violence and destruction. Personal hatred and bitterness are best exorcised, Yeats suggests, by making the self "the world's servant" (*P,* 376), through self-surrender becoming "self-possessed" (*E,* 524). Yeats's poetry in this respect can be read as a "sacred book," reflecting in its highest moments the Self-illuminating process.

In the present chapter we shall consider Yeats's "public poetry" from 1910 to 1921, concentrating on the way in which the speaker transforms his identity in the course of addressing himself to his social "responsibility." We shall consider first those poems in which the speaker makes "Helen" the paragon of nobility, and then the several poems of "exultation." "The Second Coming" will serve as our terminal point of reference.

In the "Helen" poems the old image of the immortal beloved has been replaced by the image of a woman whose mystery braves the crassness and injustice of this world. Her majestic bearing, despite her having fallen from favor, is what commends her to the speaker; and he memorializes her heroic quality while confirming his own sense of solitude. It is as though the unrequited lover had recouped his loss by sympathetic avowal of the beloved's innate dignity.

The speaker in the "Helen" poems seems to be what Yeats in *A Vision* calls "The Daimonic Man." He is a person in search of his transpersonal Self, but someone who has tried sharing the awareness of his spiritual counterpart (potentially his daimonic being) with the woman he loves. In renouncing his desire for the woman, therefore, he finds himself better able to realize his own destiny. What he is deprived of he can accept as "proof" of spiritual gain. Because he substitutes for the object of his desire a Self-inspired image, "The Daimonic Man" is obviously endowed with creative insight; but because he is in a state of transition his convictions may not be expressed with the greatest possible intensity.

> The Body of Fate [the outcome of circumstance] . . . is "loss," and works to make impossible "simplification by intensity." The being, through the intellect, selects some object of desire for a representation of the *Mask* as Image, some woman perhaps, and the *Body of Fate* snatches away the object. Then the intellect (*Creative Mind*), which in the most *antithetical* phases were better described as imagination, must substitute some new image of desire; and in the degree of its power and of its attainment of unity, relate that which is lost, that which has snatched it away, to the new image of desire, that which threatens the new image to the being's unity. (*V*, 142)

Unlike the speaker in Yeats's poems of exultation, the speaker in the "Helen" poems finds himself at cross purposes. He cannot rejoice in his vision without first arguing with himself, or with the insensitive world, for *her* sake. His grasp of his subject and its conceptual core is thus weakened because his point of view is divided. Indeed it would seem the speaker in these poems is looking for his proper subject. Consider this poem called "Words," published in 1910:

> I had this thought a while ago,
> 'My darling cannot understand
> What I have done, or what would do
> In this blind bitter land.'
>
> And I grew weary of the sun
> Until my thoughts cleared up again,
> Remembering that the best I have done
> Was done to make it plain;
>
> That every year I have cried, 'At length
> My darling understands it all,
> Because I have come into my strength,
> And words obey my call';
>
> That had she done so who can say
> What would have shaken from the sieve?
> I might have thrown poor words away
> And been content to live.

In his diary for January 22, 1909, Yeats, in talking about his twenty-year relationship with Maud Gonne, accounts for his having written this poem. "How much of the best that I have done and still do is but the attempt to explain myself to her. . . . If she understood I should lack a reason for writing and one can never have too many reasons for doing what is so laborious." [1]

Is it for her sake, for his sake, or for the sake of writing that the speaker in "Words" makes poetry of his thoughts? Each stanza turns upon a different aspect of this leading question. In stanza 1 the speaker makes ready to reassure "my darling" that he has learned to live in a country where people are "blind" and "bitter"; in stanza 2, he suggests that simply clarifying his position should be enough, making it clear to himself and her that he accepts his unequal relationship with others; and yet in stanza 3 he is dismayed that, no matter how well he reconciles himself to his situation, "my darling" will never be able to understand—him or the means by which he is able to put up with the world.

The three-way problem, then, is only partially resolved: the speaker finds strength in being able to express his thoughts about a land that otherwise would seem alien to him; but he cannot quite reconcile himself to the fact that he must live *alone* with this redeeming insight. In stanza 4 he copes with the irony only by redoubling it. Because the one person that inspires him cannot really understand him, he thinks himself cut off from life; and he thinks himself cut off because of his continuing need to express himself. He is caught in a trap of his own making, thinking that "words" would finally release him from any obsessive concern he had for those he loved or hated. But in the end "words," indeed, are all he has left, the ability to make poetry of his discontent.

When the speaker says "I might have thrown poor words away / And been content to live," he does not imply he will be satisfied living alone; he wants to be alone with his beloved, who at last would understand him. And yet the poem is not actually addressed to the beloved, as were the early love lyrics (see *P,* 157), or as was "Adam's Curse." "Words" is a discursive poem, ostensibly about a man's relationship to a woman, his compatriots, his art; but it strikes our attention more for its manner than for its specific content—the gentle, meditative tone that shows us a man struggling with his own understanding, being made to acknowledge a fate he had never asked for.

In "Words" and in other of the "Helen" poems the speaker nonetheless looks to the figure of Helen to resolve his quarrel with country and countrymen. He makes of Homer's paragon a personal example—the image of a woman who is noble enough to disregard the slights, the abuse, the intolerance, and forgetfulness of those who once held her in esteem. She is the model for the tragic joy the speaker soon after comes to feel in his own right. And from her image he soon learns to fashion a mask for himself, in the process growing more flexible in his manner of expression.

In "No Second Troy," the earliest of the "Helen" poems (1908, written, as Hone observes, after Yeats had visited Maud Gonne in Paris) the speaker takes "ignorant men" to task for not being equal to his heroine's zeal. Indignant at their common perversion of her gospel, he lauds her "most violent ways," investing her image with a nobility—"That nobleness made simple as a fire"—which consequently makes what she does of epical import.

> Why, what could she have done, being what she is?
> Was there another Troy for her to burn?

The speaker shows self-righteous anger on her behalf, not blaming her even "that she filled my days / With misery" nor attentive to that more cautious voice of the poet: Yeats himself disapproving of Maud because she gave assent to violence.[2] The speaker embraces Helen's cause with the conviction of a man who has shared her experience; and his own feelings echo as a paean to her passionate, Dianesque aloofness.

> What could have made her peaceful with a mind
> That nobleness made simple as a fire,
> With beauty like a tightened bow, a kind
> That is not natural in an age like this,
> Being high and solitary and most stern. (*P*, 256–57)

In the poem "Peace," published in series with "No Second Troy" but written a year and a half after the latter (again in relation to Yeats's visit to Maud Gonne, this time in Normandy[3]), the speaker takes a reverse stand. Instead of his headlong devotion in the earlier poem, the speaker is entirely circumspect in "Peace." He views his heroine with a more penetrating eye, modifying what he supposes to be the heroic ideal.

> Ah, that Time could touch a form
> That could show what Homer's age
> Bred to be a hero's wage.

The speaker is considerably more deliberate in his testimonial to the modern-day Helen. He is not as straightforward as he might be in his appraisal of her, but it is quite obvious that he does not condone her stormy involvement in life. It may have been that Helen's fiery temperament had been at one time commensurate with her beauty. But when Time preys on her beauty the external effects gradually are shed and what then would remain is her radiant composure. Had she indeed been as the speaker imagines, she would have served him, and those like him, as someone to emulate. Even in her youth, he conjectures, some painter might have foreseen her overwhelming virtue: her " 'delicate high head / All that sternness amid charm, / All that sweetness amid strength' " until (as was expressed in a line later deleted) " 'they had changed us to like strength. . . .' "

The speaker is no mere worshipper of feminine beauty. He is strong-willed enough to conceive of Helen as the image of what he him-

self would become. Worth noting in this respect is his attempt to iden-
tify Helen as "half lion, half child," (a therianthropic image which with
"The Second Coming" becomes a correlative for the speaker's own, transpersonal solitude and visionary insight). This composite image, as first
used in "Against Unworthy Praise," describes the unspoiled virtue of a
woman whose ideals have been misread, distorted, by unconscionable
"knaves." The speaker argues away his indignation by claiming to share
with his heroine a secret placing them above the ordinary run of men.

> O heart, be at peace, because
> Nor knave nor dolt can break
> What's not for their applause,
> Being for a woman's sake.
> Enough if the work has seemed,
> So did she your strength renew,
> A dream that a lion had dreamed
> Till the wilderness cried aloud,
> A secret between you two ["her" and his "heart"],
> Between the proud and the proud.

The speaker communes with this woman because he is assured they are,
together, in touch with the heroic world of the imagination. Their lion's
dream thus gives them strength to render ineffectual the everyday
world around them.

But just how convincing is the speaker's claim to be privy to an abiding mystery? He does not, cannot, focus squarely upon eliciting an
image from *Anima Mundi,* because his attention is divided: he is more
intent on reconciling his own differences with the world and trying to
establish at the same time the spiritual ascendancy of his heroine. The
speaker does not concentrate with the intensity of the speaker in "The
Second Coming" upon creating, or invoking, a transformational image.
The dual image of the woman—" she, singing upon her road, / Half
lion, half child"—becomes a unitive symbol only because of a juxtaposition of words, not because of any profound poetic process. As a result
the terminal figure in the poem seems merely a byproduct of the imagination and not a direct, daimonic source of inspiration.

In the sequence of poems addressed to Helen, the titular heroine is
meant to be a symbol of inner strength for having suffered defeat in the
external world. But so long as the speaker cultivates that image in its
own right, independent of his own being, and without primary emphasis upon the change he undergoes contemplating that image, he will be

able to make only minimally effective his use of image as symbol. The burden of the poem is not to prove itself a moment of stasis or to crystallize a sequence of images, but rather to suggest the poem's dynamic inscape—the power of the word to draw in toward a single symbolic center.

"The Second Coming" does this. And it appears that the transformation symbol in that poem (the sphinx) is anticipated in the "Helen" poems. "Against Unworthy Praise," written in 1910, ends with a pristine form of such a symbol. "His Phoenix" (*P,* 353–54) written four and a half years later (January 1915) makes use of an intermediate figure, a cross between the "child" and the "sphinx": "I knew a phoenix in my youth," reads the refrain; she has "the simplicity of a child. / And that proud look as though she had gazed into the burning sun [cf. "The Second Coming," l. 15], / And all the shapely body no tittle gone astray." The speaker mourns, he says, "for that most lonely thing." There is regret mixed with admiration as he recalls her untainted beauty. She had her heyday when she was young. Now she is a victim of "that barbarous crowd," isolated and alone. But her "proud look" and indomitable eye still haunt the speaker.

However, it does not seem the person speaking has gone through too great an effort to picture his phoenix. She is an image out of the immediate past,[4] not out of the larger context of *Anima Mundi.* She seems to have been born whole, not evolved through the process of the poem. Only slightly does she share in that elemental world from which the "rough beast" in "The Second Coming" originates. This latter image derives from an in-felt psychological matrix; in "His Phoenix" the speaker looks back in time, more intently than he looks within, for his controlling image.

Most of the "Helen" poems, no less than "The Second Coming," show the speaker attempting to maneuver the central image in such a way as to make it serve as a buffer between himself and his outrage—a solvent for the indignant attitude he has toward "the barbarous crowd." In "The People" (*P,* 351–53), written at about the same time as "His Phoenix," and published together with that poem and five others in *Poetry,* February 1916, the speaker engages his transfigured heroine in a dialogue concerning the people. Unlike other of the "Helen" poems, this is a poem of self-reproof. The man who has spent a good part of his life working for "this unmannerly town" questions the value of his sacrifice. He might as well have given in to his tendency to withdraw from the thankless world, he says, and move instead "among the images of the past / . . . unperturbed and courtly images" of Quattrocento Italy "where the Duchess and her people talked / The stately midnight through until they stood / In their great window looking at the dawn." But that kind of intellectual and esthetic isolation is only a halfway house, his twentieth-century lady tells him. There are those, of course—the "drunkards, pilferers of public funds"—who thrive upon dishonesty, but do they constitute "the people," she asks, do they make up the real body of the country? Despite what wrong had been done her, she tells him, " 'never have I, now nor at any time, Complained of the people.' " He counters the simplicity of her faith. She is ruled by her heart, he says, not by any "analytic mind." And then he recoils from his words. Meeting his indignation head-on, her generosity puts him to shame. He suddenly recognizes the truth of her words.[5]

The "Helen" poems contrast markedly with the early poems of exultation, in that the latter are more directly concerned with the self-illuminating intensity of the speaking voice. They seem indeed the antithetical counterparts of the "Helen" poems—visionary rather than devotional in manner. Let us examine now the poems of exultation and determine in what way they, like the "Helen" poems, anticipate the premonitory tone of "The Second Coming."

"Life is not lived," Yeats wrote in 1907, "if not lived for contemplation or excitement" (*E,* 252). Visionary excitement indeed may be induced by contemplation. The contemplative mind is able to symbolize, intensify by simplifying its comprehension of reality, and as a result grow free of nonessential impressions. It is different from the "analytic mind" which multiplies by dividing in that it tends to magnify partial aspects of reality into representations of the whole: coloring what it sees with its own bias.

Tom O'Roughley, the titular figure of a poem Yeats wrote in 1918, focuses upon the differences between the two states of mind: "Wisdom is a butterfly," he says, "and not a gloomy bird of prey." The analytic mind feeds upon rather than frees itself of the world—imposes meaning, sets goals, establishes rules, in short, perpetuates by delimiting its range of reference. "Logic-choppers rule the town" is how Tom sums it up. But Tom does not bank upon the wayward world for his direction in life: " 'An aimless joy is a pure joy,' " he says. And to show his joyous indifference, he turns a lively heel upon all speculation concerning life and death:

'If little planned is little sinned
But little need the grave distress.
What's dying but a second wind?
How but in zig-zag wantonness
Could trumpeter Michael be so brave?'
Or something of that sort he said,
'And if my dearest friend were dead
I'd dance a measure on his grave.' (*P, 337–38*)

The linear movement of the poem, accelerating to its final statement by rhetorical questioning, accords nicely with Tom's startling final gesture, his gay dismissal of any speculative faith. His attitude is not unlike that of Yeats writing in 1907: "That we may be free from . . . sullen anger, solemn virtue, calculating anxiety, gloomy suspicion, prevaricating hope, we should be reborn in gaiety" (*E, 252*). Tom envisions his own transformation: and his espousal of a "zig-zag wantonness" seems a felicitous correlative of the speaker's visionary excitement.

Tom has the last word, but we wonder if the author has not after all been overly deliberate in structuring the poem, in writing about his sense of exultation and in using the too mindful indirection of a persona. The more characteristic of Yeats's poems feature the first-person narrator, who makes us feel the immediacy of his subject.

In "The Dawn," similar in theme to "Tom O'Roughley," the speaker contemplates directly his subject and then rises to the full strength of his controlling image. The ironic first eight lines, telescoping the world he takes exception to, prevent any progressive concentration of mood; but the lines nonetheless seem to provide a springboard for his excitement, as reflected in the culminating image.

I would be ignorant as the dawn
That has looked down
On that old queen measuring a town
With the pin of a brooch,
Or on the withered men that saw
From their pedantic Babylon
The careless planets in their courses,
The stars fade out where the moon comes,
And took their tablets and did sums;
I would be ignorant as the dawn
That merely stood, rocking the glittering coach
Above the cloudy shoulders of the horses;
I would be—for no knowledge is worth a straw—
Ignorant and wanton as the dawn.

Again (*cf.* "Tom O'Roughley") the speaker expresses his desire to be free of that peddling intellect which can "measure a town" or reduce to a piece of slate the incalculable mystery of the cosmos. The speaker holds thumbs down on products of the analytic mind, himself having recourse to the larger, yet self-contained, world of the imagination.

> I would be ignorant as the dawn
> That merely stood, rocking the glittering coach
> Above the cloudy shoulders of the horses. . . .

His insight takes the form of an image of static intensity, signifying, as he hopes, his would-be transformation.

Yeats used over and again the images of animals and "dawn" to express the consecrated energy of the moment of vision. It is not until the very late poem "High Talk" that the speaker blends these images into the perfect climax for a poem of exultation (see pp. 150 ff. below): but we may profitably pause, I think, over the use of these images in the earlier poems. In "The Dawn" the conjunction of horses and sun is perhaps the most memorable composite image of transfiguration in Yeats's early poetry. In three other poems, all written before "The Dawn"—"At Galway Races" (1908), "Upon a House shaken by the Land Agitation" (1909), and the poem to which Yeats gave his longest title, "To a Wealthy Man who promised a Second Subscription to the Dublin Municipal Gallery if it were proved the People wanted Pictures" (1912)— we have the visionary images of horse and sun dealt with separately. We might look at these three poems before passing on to the more emotionally ambivalent poems of exultation.

Unlike the narration in "Tom O'Roughley," "The Dawn," and other later poems describing the speaker's elation, the narrator in these three early poems rides dauntlessly high because of his sense of aristocratic pride. "At Galway Races," the first of Yeats's poems of exultation, shows the narrator boldly articulating his triumphal vision. The spectacle of the race is regarded as the spirit of the country as a whole, the brave riders setting an example for the people to follow:

> There where the course is,
> Delight makes all of the one mind,
> The riders upon the galloping horses,
> The crowd that closes in behind. . . .

There is not a bit of scorn in the speaker's words. His optimism rings with the sense of *noblesse oblige*. With "horsemen for companions" he may look down on "the merchant and the clerk," but nonetheless holds out some hope for their redemption. All life, he supposes, can be refashioned from the vision of "men / That ride upon horses." And their concerted response to an apocalyptic trumpeting is what sustains the imagination of such men:

> Sing on: somewhere at some new moon,
> We'll learn that sleeping is not death,
> Hearing the whole world change its tune,
> Its flesh being wild. . . .

No feeling of separation or defeat here. The vibrant tread of horsemen is meant to be felt in this stirring image of a world potentially transformed.

In "At Galway Races" there are foreshadowings of "The Second Coming," but the buoyant tone of this early poem is a far cry from the probative vision of the speaker in the later poem. For all his gallantry the speaker in "At Galway Races" cultivates too broad a view, extending himself without sufficient check upon his imagination: he seems hellbent on a vision of unity-of-being among all men. And this vision, the poet realizes later, is impossible (*A*, 235–36). The relation of man to men is too problematic to allow the visionary anything finally but the promise of his own solitude.

A new note is sounded in a poem Yeats wrote a year after "At Galway Races": it is addressed to Lady Gregory, who numbered among the last of Ireland's landed aristocracy. Quizzically the speaker asks:

> How should the world be luckier if this house,
> Where passion and precision have been one
> Time out of mind, became too ruinous
> To breed the lidless eye that loves the sun?

The speaker is concerned with the problem of preserving from destruction the invaluable emblems of nobility. The external effects (the material dwelling) may become common property, he says, but that will never endow the new owners with the character of the people the dwelling once housed; and how can the actual possession ever compare with the spiritual resolve of those who had lived there? Yet, however much the speaker regrets the fall of the physical structure, he wonders if its demolition will really keep the tradition from being perpetuated. It should, he supposes, serve only to inure the spirit, allow the self-liberating mind to discover above all else "gradual Time's last gift," what no man of mean wealth can ever understand: "a written speech / Wrought of high laughter, loveliness and ease." The noble mind finds in lofty repose enduring strength: "sweet laughing eagle thoughts that grow / Where wings have memory of wings, and all / That comes of the best knit to the best." The proud heights inherited by "the best" are those "eagle thoughts" signified by the hieratic symbol of the "eye that loves the sun."

In "To a Wealthy Man . . ." the sun's eye is a symbol for those aspiring to be remembered among "the best."

> Let Paudeens play at pitch and toss,
> Look up in the sun's eye and give
> What the exultant heart calls good
> That some new day may breed the best
> Because you gave, not what they would,
> But the right twigs for an eagle's nest!

"Eagle" and "sun" are matched in dignity, symbols of an aristocratic pride. But they are not symbols entirely pared of reference to the material world; the speaker is asking the wealthy man to give money (in spite of the money-minded Paudeens) in order to further the cause of art. Art, "whose end is peace," would presumably set the proper tone for the city and, in its conspicuous stillness, would seem to triumph over the rankling crowd.

It was a year before the speaker would address another patron of the arts and assure her that noble souls are "Bred to a harder thing / Than Triumph." He advised her to "take defeat": "turn away / And like a laughing string / Whereon mad fingers play / . . . Be secret and exult, / Because of all things known / That is most difficult" (*P,* 291).

The speaker comes around to acknowledging that the real challenge for the beleaguered soul is to evolve a discipline of laughter, feeding elation not on splendiferous visions or bright arrays of possibility but on the more salient issue of broken hopes and unrealized dreams. What's desired is the free feeling that comes of having been purged of personal bitterness, indignation, and pride. It is a humbling and a revelation, the shock of illumination in the wilderness, a stigmatic release of emotion.

The three poems which most aptly convey the mixture of pain and elation, "Paudeen," "The Cold Heaven," and "Demon and Beast," contrast
therefore in tone with the three "aristocratic" poems of exultation. And
they contrast as well with "The Dawn" and "Tom O'Roughley," poems
in which the innocence and quicksilver quality of the speaker prevail.

In the three, what we may call "stigmatic" poems of exultation, the
speaker traverses an emotional spectrum from pain, indignation, or
hatred, to self-enlightenment.[6] He is lifted, it seems, in the process of
transcribing his vision. In "Paudeen" and "The Cold Heaven" the cumulative excitement of the words virtually imitates the ecstatic heighten-
ing that the speaker professes to undergo. With the culminating moment in each poem something flashes upon the mind's eye of the
speaker, an image shivering with visionary intensity. The image of the
sun, evident in most of the poems we are considering, in these two
poems seems to show through an inner light, refulgent with the speaker's own articulate energy.

> Indignant at the fumbling wits, the obscure spite
> Of our old Paudeen in his shop, I stumbled blind
> Among the stones and thorn-trees, under morning light;
> Until a curlew cried and in the luminous wind
> A curlew answered; and suddenly thereupon I thought
> That on the only height where all are in God's eye,
> There cannot be, confusion of our thought forgot,
> A single soul that lacks a sweet crystalline cry. (*P*, 291)

> . . . And I took all the blame out of all sense and reason,
> Until I cried and trembled and rocked to and fro,
> Riddled with light.[7]   (*P*, 316)

In both poems, as well as in "Demon and Beast," the image of the
birds helps bring about a catalytic change in the speaker. It is significant
that in none of these poems do we get the proud image of hawk or
eagle. They are common birds—the curlew, the rook,[8] the gull or "some
absurd / Portly green-pated bird"—which touch upon the speaker's emotions, filling him at once with remorse and joy; for him the sight of
them, their free-flying and yet humble forms, induces tears that are
gladly shed, feelings which whelm up when grievance gives way to forgiveness and pride dissolves in benediction. "Being no more demoniac /
A stupid happy creature / Could rouse my whole nature" (*P*, 400).

The conflict described in these three poems is the conflict between a

man's demonic and daimonic natures. The speaker's quarrel with the
world can result only in disdain or hate, or else erupt in some act of violence; but if the quarrel is contained and the self becomes the principal
target of the speaker, then the latter is able to project over and beyond
any demonic assertion the mystery of his spiritual Daimon.

The stigmatic poems are the outcome of this recurrent struggle, the
moment of poetic vision translating the emotional experience. The
speaker can celebrate his triumph because he has found momentary release from his shadow—the selfish, delimiting aspect of his being. The
dissociated images of beast and bird are thus used to describe an un-
winding, "contraconic," experience: the way antipathetic (animal-spirit-
ual) elements are resolved through enlightened understanding of the
self and others. The idea is expressed in the opening lines of "Demon
and Beast"—

> For certain minutes at the least
> That crafty demon and that loud beast
> That plague me day and night
> Ran out of my sight;
> Though I had long perned in the gyre,
> Between my hatred and my desire,
> I saw my freedom won
> And all laugh in the sun.

This first stanza ends with reference to the sun as an image of unfet-
tered happiness; the next stanza is concerned with the manifestation of
an inner light.

The speaker finds himself in the "sweet company" of dead men, por-
traits that speak out to him the vital wisdom of *Anima Mundi*. Having
comprehended those nodding and smiling figures on the wall—"glittering eyes in a death's head"—he is able to rout the blatant "beast" and
thereby feel the spiritual purity which makes him at one with all men:
"For all men's thoughts grew clear / Being dear as mine are dear." His
understanding now is of the heart as well as the head, and presumably
he resolves for the moment that antinomy which, in "The People,"
keeps the speaker from realizing the possible "purity of a natural force"
("his phoenix's" unconditional belief in "the people").

The speaker's humanity is not proved until a pervading joy is able to
make him surrender his intellectual and egotistic pride. That done, his
example might serve the people: for "never yet had freeman / Right

mastery of natural things." For the speaker freedom is evidenced by passionate self-control, and once the demon has been exorcised, that freedom allows a more profound sensitivity. His entire being is engaged by two "stupid happy creatures"—a gyring gull splashing down beside a floating duck. The birds express for him "aimless joy" and bring "a tear-drop" to his eye. Apparently he feels the release that comes from a sudden conjunction of opposites, the felicitous melding of instinct and insight. For the moment his "whole nature" responds to the world around him with primordial innocence.

The speaker thus discovers the exquisite "sweetness" of life, having "no dearer thought / Than . . . [to] find out a way / To make it linger half a day." A man's life, though, is necessarily bound by a self-conscious existence; as a result the natural world is seen at its purest only when death is regarded, not as an ironic or absurd fate, but as a means of spiritual release—

> O what a sweetness strayed
> Through the barren Thebaid,
> Or by the Mareotic sea
> When that exultant Anthony
> And twice a thousand more
> Starved upon the shore
> And withered to a bag of bones!
> What had the Caesars but their thrones?

The life of Saint Anthony is interpreted by what Yeats in "Phase 27" of *A Vision* calls the "Emotion of Sanctity," the realization of a "contact with life beyond death." "It comes," Yeats maintains, "when synthesis [of facts and ideas] is abandoned, when fate is accepted" above the strictures of reason and intellect.

The vision of Anthony exulting at his death consummates the sequence of images (i.e., light-sight-liquid images) in this discursive poem. It completes the experience of the speaker whom we see first "laughing in the sun," then communing with "glittering eyes in a death's head," finally feeling "a tear-drop start . . . up" as he watches a bird by "the little lake . . . take / A bit of bread. . . ." Like the saint of "Phase 27" the speaker seems to allow "the total life, expressed in its humanity, to flow in upon him and to express itself through his acts and thoughts." What the speaker sees, thinks, and does thus makes for a composite emotion, reflecting his understanding of that extraordinary scene "by the Mareotic sea."

The poem, worked out in terms of this daimonic vision of Saint Anthony, is the last of Yeats's three stigmatic poems of exultation. It is a fitting conclusion to the cycle. The contritional intensity of "Paudeen" and "The Cold Heaven" is relaxed in "Demon and Beast"; the moment of revelation is extended in such a way as to allow the speaker to comprehend the human condition, the "total life" clarified for him in the emotion aroused by a sympathetic, because transpersonal, awareness.

We have considered thus far groups of poems which describe a progressive internalization of image. The "Helen" series, which succeeds the adorational and apocalyptic love lyrics of the early years, projects the heroic ideal of the poet in the image of a woman; the heroine has an almost divine nobility, and is endowed with spiritual beauty. In the poems of exultation it is the speaker himself who commands our attention; and the key images in the poem are those which reveal the nature of his spiritual state. Like "The Gift of Harun Al-Raschid," the last of the marital love poems, the early poems of exultation conclude with the figural representation of a mysterious (daimonic) reality. The stigmatic poems differ from the other poems of exultation, as well as from the "Helen" poems, the marital love poems, and the spiritual and sensuous love lyrics, in that they express a more embracing, human love; the speaker is shown struggling to overcome the daimonic pride and hatred that plagues the soul; and, as we have seen, he emerges from the struggle with a more charitable vision of mankind—a brand of social "responsibility" which allows him to "respond" to, and by this means accept, the human condition as a measure of his personal effort at Self-fulfillment.[9]

A man's actions, Yeats realized, should relate to his social "responsibility." If hatred is "the common condition of our life," as he says in the essay "Anima Mundi" (*M, 365*), then it must be consciously controlled. The demon cannot be thought merely to have run away in a moment of enlightenment. The struggle for self-mastery is wholly internal, and it continues as long as there is one's self to think about.

The ideal that makes life livable cannot be conceived to lie outside the human mind. It is a self-sustaining force. "When I remember that Shelley calls our minds 'mirrors of the fire for which all thirst,' I cannot but ask the question all have asked, 'What or who has cracked the mirror?' I begin to study the only self that I can know, myself, and to wind the thread upon the pern again" (*M, 364*). It is when the mind fastens upon some reality beyond itself that the "thread" is likely to snap and thereby scotch the vision of life. Unlike Shelley, Yeats learned to take the living world for proof of his own intensity, and not consider it merely a perversion of reality. Because, as Yeats claimed in his essay "Anima Mundi," a poem could be its own revelation (once the imagination burned free of self-consciousness), then the world itself, from which the poem is drawn, would seem a revelation: it would be allowed its own rhythm, coexisting, curiously enough, with the unresolved images of *Anima Mundi,* the "soul of the world" which haunts the visionary mind.

The vision for Yeats is its own solvent, reducing to a common denominator seemingly disparate images. "I look at the strangers near," Yeats reports in describing this state of mind, "as if I had known them all my life. . . : everything fills me with affection, I have no longer any fears or any needs." And he goes on to explain, in the essay "Anima Mundi," that this affection makes him susceptible to the intelligence of some higher being, casting for him a mysterious image. (The kind of autochthonous love Yeats describes here, one may note, is the antithesis of Shelley's ethereal, Platonic love.)

> I have something about me that, though it makes me love, is more like innocence. I am in the place where the Daimon is, but I do not think he is with me until I begin to make a new personality, selecting among those images, seeking always to satisfy a hunger grown out of conceit with daily diet; and yet as I write the words 'I select,' I am full of uncertainty, not knowing when I am the finger, when the clay. Once, twenty years ago, I seemed to awake from sleep to find my body rigid, and to hear a strange voice speaking these words through my lips as through lips of stone: 'We make an image of him who sleeps, and it is not he who sleeps, and we call it Emmanuel.' (*M,* 365–66)

The image Yeats talks about, no less than the condition attending its inception, anticipates the visionary image effected in "The Second Coming." "Emmanuel," Hebrew for "God be with us," is meant by Yeats to signify not the messianic figure of a man, as the Old Testament tradition would have it, but an unconscious presence. At the critical moment between sleeping and waking, when the subconscious weighs in often precarious balance with the conscious mind, the ghostly voice all but paralyzes personal will, and projects upon the subliminal imagination the unsatisfied will of the dead; the body becomes a suspended form, transfigured momentarily by atavistic images impressed upon the mind.

"The Second Coming," written about eighteen months after "Anima

Mundi," objectifies an autohypnotic state, showing the speaker in the process of eliciting from *Spiritus Mundi* the transformational image. More so than any previous lyric, even the three stigmatic poems, "The Second Coming" demonstrates what Yeats meant by "responsibility." The speaker "responds" transpersonally to the threat of destruction. A cool intensity replaces the "wild" excitement and elated agony of the early poems of exultation. Anarchic events are accepted as manifestations of man's impending fate; they are not regarded simply as a challenge to the speaker's defense of an heroic order. Aristocratic pride, personal bitterness, indignation toward the ungovernable crowd no longer are the vital issues. Prophetic insight has more than offset the prospect of social upheaval.[10]

There is an apparent reversal in the point of view of the poem. The dissolving center of the phenomenal reality gives way to a startling image of concentration so that, as a result, the centrifugal demon seems to have been brought under control of a daimonic intelligence. The animal form that slowly evolves in the mind's eye—an organic, yet entelic, energy—heralds, therefore, the watchful release of the body. The speaker may thus be said to have struck a radical balance, evoking the symbol of a potentially interchangeable (physical-spiritual) reality.

That unformed image of the beast was formerly contained by the unconscious, confined by—but now, under the aspect of violence—ready to break from, any rational order.[11] And from the cultural devotion of the past twenty centuries, it would appear, will emerge for the uninitiated a subterranean terror; for the visionary that terror, however, is subliminal, and may be brought to light not in fear but out of a complementary, immanent wisdom. The manifestation of force would seem to breed a vision of final destruction; but for the speaker it becomes an occasion for spiritual revelation, bringing on a flash of insight which intimates a change, gradual and deliberate, as natural as the mystery of any emerging form. It is a psychogenic emancipation. And it is made possible through metamorphosis, not through any retaliatory exchange of power. Any action in the external world, as Schopenhauer claimed, will have served to mirror back upon the doer the extravagant energy of his own will, forcing the individual to recognize the self, and not some outside power, as the unpurged source of evil in the world.

The contemplative vision results from surrender of the will. It leads to dissolution of the energy of the self by dissolving into daimonic symbol images which have taken hold on the mind and whose assertive force has not yet been exhausted. Symbolic form results from a concen-tration which purifies by relaxing the conscious mold of organic form: breaking up (without destroying its reticulate core) any rigidified, spe-cific pattern of thought. Under the influence of its own generative power, mind and body operate more equally upon each other, re-forming the self, making it progressively less insistent upon proving its will upon other selves, other forms of being. Once circumstances in the surround-ing world can be accepted as its own fate, then the self enlarges its ca-pacity for being.

In this consists the commanding mystery and solitude of the vision-ary. In "The Second Coming" the speaker appears to have let himself be overshadowed by his image of the sphinx, allowing it to proliferate, by religious and historical association, while converging toward an instinc-tive unity, the elemental ground of the imagination. The living-stone is assigned no specified locale; the sands of the desert, suggesting the slow passing of time, become a correlative for the ineffectual world the stone image will displace; but that image takes shape as a phantasmagoria, calculated to rephrase the historical question in the form of a spiritual enigma: "what rough beast . . .?"

It is curious that none of the existing critiques of "The Second Com-ing" have focused squarely upon the state of mind of the speaker. What the poem says about the world and beast is not meant as simply a projection of the formidable state of affairs today, and the prospect of some equally formidable antidote. With the above discussion I have been suggesting that the poem be read as proof of the speaker's journey toward psychological equanimity. The images, while certainly gathered from the real world (history and culture), reflect control of an inner world, the untried recesses of the self. And again, unlike previous critics of the poem, I take for my verifying text "Phase 22" of *A Vision*: the pivotal point in the transition from the subjective to the ghostly self.[12] In "Phase 22," Yeats muses, "we seem to have renounced our ambition under the influence of some strange, far-reaching impartial gaze." The evolving image of the sphinx returns just this kind of impartial gaze— "blank and pitiless as the sun" (the most memorable perhaps of Yeats' eye-sun images): its indifferent wisdom seeming to confront us with the inherent justice of man's fate. However the world may fare, a man's ac-ceptance of his "responsibility" makes available to him the redeeming strength of his imagination. He may "use the *Body of Fate* to deliver the *Creative Mind* from the *Mask* [Yeats describes this as "self-

immolation"] . . . , so using the intellect upon the facts of the world
that the last vestige of personality disappears." At this point "the desire
to dominate has so completely vanished, 'amalgamation' [the resolving
power of the imagination] has pushed its way into the subconscious,
into that which is dark, that we call it a vision." The man of action is
the antithesis of the visionary; he cannot internalize his sense of mission,
he cannot amalgamate through art or language what he feels must be
expressed. Action, Yeats observes, "is a form of abstraction that crushes
everything it cannot express." "Men will die and murder for an abstract
synthesis, and the more abstract it is the further it carries them from
compunction and compromise; and as obstacles to that synthesis increase, the violence of their will increases. . . . Before the point of balance has been reached" [the moment of vision] a man who is "out of
phase" (yet identified with "Phase 22") may "become a destroyer and
persecutor, a figure of tumult and of violence." The imaginative mind
confronts such a demonstration of self, opposing to license and havoc a
spiritual vision which is ominous, appalling. But before some actual Ar-
mageddon, it is visionary insight which is most instructive: "life, the balance reached, becomes [for men of "Phase 22"] an act of contemplation.
There is no longer a desired object, as distinct from thought itself, no
longer a *Will,* as distinct from the process of nature seen as fact. . . . Intellect knows itself as its own object of desire; and the *Will* knows itself
to be the world" (*V,* 157–63).

Individuation triangulates itself into self, spirit, world; it is the conscious separation of a spiritual whole. Not until the self foresees its identity with the world and can so refine its desire as to understand the troubled soul of the world—the residual consciousness of "Anima Mundi"—
not until then will the imagination be able to conjure any embracing vision of reality.

The sphinx may offer only a glimpse of the underlying truth, but its
momentary appearance is sufficiently edifying. The poet submits his will
to the innervating fire of his imagination. No longer is he content with
the prefigured beatitude of heroic Helen, "his phoenix," "half-child," fit
to be despoiled, perhaps, by a centaur; nor, after 1913, is he moved to
scale terrestrial heights, raising his voice in the *peine et joie* of illumination. In "The Second Coming" the poet's imagination is felt to move
through the image, the speaker's voice vibrant with the intimation of
something a part of, though mysteriously removed from, himself.

The unconscious is rendered in "The Second Coming" in terms of common experience, half-revealed, but shared on our part by some twinge of recognition. Coupled with that strange, lurking image of the beast is the guiding hand of the speaker, holding in counterpoise the claims of personal assertion and social violence. The speaker braces with the threat of utter destruction a petrifying construct of the psyche—so that as a result the cause of man's inhumanity is made over into a millennial symbol of transformation. That symbol for the moment obliterates all attention to the images which circumscribe it—images of blood, water, sun, stone, sand. The *trompe l'oeil* of the sphinx moving impresses itself upon the mind with the sudden curtain-drop, followed by the speaker's unresolved question at the end. And the shadow of that harrowing beast seems to linger after the last words in the poem are spoken.

chapter 6

the destructive vision and "Leda and the swan"

In "The Second Coming" the speaker acknowledges his responsibility to a culture of which he, his compatriots, and the illustrious dead of *Anima Mundi* are all a part. By sounding out his own spiritual potential, the speaker seems to be challenging the psychology of human violence, and, in the reflective guise of a demigod, indifferently involved in man's fate, he holds up to us the Gorgonian face of man.

The speaker has indeed come a long way in his dialogue with reality. His quest for ultimate integrity takes him beyond the transeunt effectiveness of love and beauty; his desire for spiritual, sensuous, or marital union with the beloved has served only to leave him in solitary union with "what is permanent in the soul of the world" (*E*, 286). As though to counterpoint the reaching love, the heroic pride, the exultant joy expressed in earlier poems, the speaker in "The Second Coming" gives himself over entirely to his source of vision. He is consequently able to draw from the collective unconscious an objective image of the demiurge, dormant in us all, warning of the violent outcome of unvoiced passion.

Since conceiving *A Vision*, Yeats aimed to bring himself closer to the center of life, finding through order of the imagination the means to comprehend psychological antinomies. Writing to Lady Gregory, January 4, 1918, he declares he has become suddenly receptive to a "very profound, very exciting mystical philosophy—which seems the fulfilment of many dreams and prophecies"; it "makes me feel that for the first time," he said, "I understand human life." This feeling, he finds, makes him subject to "a strange sense of revelation," a state of mind which becomes expressed in writing as "intricate passion" (*L*, 643–44). It is a form of tension attempting to circumscribe world and self, and in this way place into narrowing opposition subjective and objective modes of being. Opposition of this kind constitutes the very pulse of life, a movement in nature, in history, in the human mind which ceases only when "all life would cease" (*Ex,* 305).

Everything finally can be reduced to a "history of the mind," as Yeats told Dorothy Wellesley. One tries to plumb reality by plunging more and more deeply into the "madness of vision." That way, Yeats explains, lies some understanding of the relationship between "separated things" (*L,* 887). The soul extends and returns to itself in a constant attempt to be free, liberated even from the need to be free. This is what Yeats meant in talking of freedom and surrender as alternate moments in the dialectic of self and soul: "I am always, in all I do, driven to a moment which is the realisation of myself as unique and free, or to a moment which is the surrender to God of all that I am" (*Ex,* 305). In shifting continually from the former to the latter mood a man feels, increasingly, a need to become "the world's servant."

In the constant interchange between world and self, self and God, is the process of enlightenment. No man is wholly "subjective" or wholly "objective," in-going or out-going, in his attempt to order reality, but in his psychological makeup one or the other tendency preponderates. Yeats paraphrased very neatly the terms of this dichotomy: "All men with subjective natures move towards a possible ecstasy, all with objective natures towards a possible wisdom" (*L,* 917). From his own testimony in *The Autobiography* we would assume that Yeats was the "subjective" type, and that his predisposition toward "mystic philosophy" and ecstatic revelations quite naturally complemented his introspective bias.

But this is only partly true. Though Yeats had mystical tendencies he never felt he was a mystic (*L,* 921). The visionary state, Yeats felt, if indeed initiated in ecstasy, would eventually lead to "objective wisdom." "The Second Coming" is a notable case in point: presumably the speaker is possessed by his vision, but the vision is derived from and returns the speaker to the condition of the world around him; we may imagine that as a result of a visionary excitement the poet is able to synthesize from impressions, observations, and contemplation an appropriate psychohistorical symbol, and from this synthesis in turn he can effectively apply his deeper understanding of cultural evolution.

The pure concentration of energy demanded in moments of ecstasy has always to give way, perhaps exhaust that energy. It may be that this will reverse the unitive and the abstracting process peculiar to the visionary, leaving, according to Yeats, a world "where all shall [be] as particular and concrete as human intensity permits" (*Ex,* 305).

The spiritual tendency, then, rather than hoarding up its gains in an envisioned paradise, can be so redirected as to return the self closer to the mainstream of life; but with this difference—that the self is finally emancipated from its illusions of freedom, separation, defeat, or victory. An expansive though solitary self-knowledge turns out to be the visionary's principal reward. Even thoughts of an afterlife Yeats tends to regard as an endless refinement of this knowledge. As Graham Hough has so aptly put it:

> What is peculiar to Yeats is that the discarnate existence [as described in Book II of *A Vision*] is filled with a repetition of what has already happened in the flesh, a continuation of its passion, even its relations with other beings. So that the whole myth takes the form of an indefinite extension of the phenomenal world, as though it were that which Yeats wishes to make eternal.[1]

The eternal moment, approachable through vision, thus may be said to harbor always the possibility of its temporal resolution. This is the paradox that applies not only to Yeats's spiritual life but to his poetry as well.

It is now a commonplace to assert that Yeats's work becomes continually more concrete in conception, its syntax more rigorous, its images more sharply defined; but we must remember that this tendency reflects the poet's firmer grasp of the spiritual, not the material, content of life. Throughout we have noted the contrary themes which go to make up Yeats's poetry: the antimony between mortal and immortal love, self and Daimon, Daimon and world. These are aspects of a tension which serves continually to refocus, sharpen the spiritual vision: all to bring about a more substantial understanding of reality. We shall concentrate presently on the two categories in this dialectical tension which seem most applicable to the final phase of Yeats's writing: his alternately "subjective" and "objective" response to reality. This involves us in discussion of his poetry of ecstasy ("Byzantium" and "High Talk"), his poetry of wisdom ("Lapis Lazuli," *Meditations in Times of Civil War*), poetry which is a composite of wisdom and ecstasy ("Among School Children," "Leda and the Swan," "The Statues"), and poetry which results from a collapse of vision and ends in the reflexion of wisdom ("The Circus Animals' Desertion").

In considering poems of the late period it is important to keep in mind what Yeats postulated as the endpoint of spiritual-esthetic development. The endpoint is the hypothetical center of reality, the resolution, impossible as long as there is life, of the dichotomy of self and Self, the psychological seesaw of subjective being and objective insight. There is a constant alternation, but the tendency is to be somehow rid of the self, and to become wholly "objective" in one's response to life.[2] Granted such an ultimate stage is impossible, it can nonetheless be described. Mind and body, thought and image, dissolve into each other. The hypothetical Self, a sort of universal Daimon, entirely without personality, is able to contain by being completely receptive to all other selves. If such a psychophysiological state were possible, so too would be the absolute poem. This would be a wordless, transparent, utterly lucid form, free of every conceivable kind of assertion. Because there would be "complete passivity," there would be "complete plasticity" (*V*, 183).

Ultimate truth is spiritual life without limit or qualification. To be in a position to see that "objective" truth, one must have been able to run the gamut of "subjective" experience, putting into viable form what one hopes to be free of. "Mankind must be seen and understood in every possible circumstance, in every conceivable situation," Yeats claimed in 1908. "There is no laughter too bitter, no irony too harsh for utterance, no passion too terrible to be set off before the minds of men."[3] The poet is thus able to reduce by an act of the mind the assertive act, the embittering experience. A man's will can then change by redefining its object, seeking, not outside, but within to satisfy any formative passion. "We must love, man, woman, or child, we must exhaust ambition, intellect, desire, dedicating all things as they pass." (*E*, 483).

Artistic energy is "a conflagration of all the energies of active life" (*E*, 277). The creative imagination is an in-forming energy, seeking order, to be sure,[4] but no external unity. The poet, through his "new form of philosophy," can begin to accept the world in accepting his own fate, finding that sufficient and "good" which he can "contemplate as doing always and no other doing at all."[5] For Yeats, the poetic creation, for all its painstaking labor, is the sort of task he would have wished to make eternal. The function of the soul is alternately to transcend forms and to create forms (*L*, 403), establishing the poet's faith as that which does not ask for ultimate release. Yeats gradually came to believe with his father that poetry is a sacred book of the secular spirit, and that "the world won't be right till poetry is made life itself."[6] Though indeed he may have seemed to vacillate in his commitment, speculating about that "ultimate reality" in which "all movement, all thought, all perception [is] extinguished" (*Ex,* 307), he quite obviously took the direction in which "life itself" was leading him. "There is nothing but life," he would aver (*L,* 728). "One never tires of life and at the last must die of thirst with the cup at one's lip" (*L,* 711).

It was in this spirit that he insisted that life attempt to consume itself. This was the purpose of the ecstatic vision, the means by which an objective understanding of man would eventually be possible. Earlier he had wished the world itself consumed, destroyed because it stood between himself and the realization of his love. Later he would have the martyred hero of *The Unicorn from the Stars* declare, at his moment of greatest excitement, that "it was but a frenzy . . . going out to burn and destroy. . . . The battle we have to fight is fought out in our own mind." He thus conceives of "the fiery moment" when heaven blazes in on the mind as "the joy of Heaven, continual battle" (*PL,* 243–45). Martin, the hero, sees the afterlife as continuous with the penultimate terms of this life, when the senses are continually turned inward and "there is nothing"—nothing in the external world—to delude us as we satisfy our passion.

Those mysterious musicians at the end of the later play *The Resurrection* speak of Christ's revelation in conjunction with the cleansing flame of self-destruction:

> Everything that man esteems
> Endures a moment or a day:
> Love's pleasure drives his love away,
> The painter's brush consumes his dreams;
> The herald's cry, the soldier's tread
> Exhaust his glory and his might:
> Whatever flames upon the night
> Man's own resinous heart has fed. (*PL,* 373)

A man's task is "to pierce . . . the wild heart of time," (*PL,* 243) igniting the pyre of his own, little world. By this means he may so exhaust pride and passion that his spiritual consummation will have left him no less than a refined, transpersonal wisdom. In writing to Sturge Moore, Yeats proposes that man's greatness is evidenced only in "a series of sudden fires" and that we are liberated in the degree we diminish the tendentious ladders of time. Via moments of vision "we free ourselves that we may be nothing" (*YM,* 154).[7]

The vigor increasingly characteristic of Yeats's poetry is meant to disestablish the validity of the external form. The hand fashioning the poem delimits the claims of the self, recreating what was seen with the visible eye or what was simply thought or dreamed to be the incontrovertible reality. The self subsists as long as thought or imagination are at work, so that the finished form, whether material or esthetic, can be conceived only as another limitation imposed by the outside world. "If our works could / But vanish with our breath / That were a lucky death," declares the speaker in "Nineteen Hundred and Nineteen" (*P,* 431). It is only the image resisting conscious formulation, the knowledge that is not preconceived, which binds the self to its proper study, making the daimonic—rather than any extrinsic—tension paramount in the poem and the creative process.

"I seek an image, not a book," says Ille in the dialogue "Ego Dominus Tuus." He implies that the written work is no more than a means, the mask that attempts to tighten upon the mystery impelling toward articulation. The work is nothing ever complete, to be understood apart from an intuitive knowledge of reality. "Those men that in their writings are most wise / Own nothing but their blind, stupefied hearts." For Yeats the written word is sacred only if it suggests what in itself is ineffable, that spirit that must continually be urged into being:

> I call to the mysterious one who yet
> Shall walk the wet sands. . . .

This being is the imagined counterpart of the speaker, intimating to him what to others cannot be communicated. It is the spiritual opposite of the speaker, "My anti-self," whose mystery necessarily depends upon some future revelation; it is the substantive reality, a secret knowledge, which wholly transforms the self, and yet would betray the meaning of life were it made fully known "before it is dawn" (*P,* 370–71).

Writing in 1906 to Florence Farr, Yeats makes report of the critical change he feels has come into his life and work. This change meant for him a new comprehension of image and reality:

> I feel this change in all my work and that it has brought
> a change into the personal relations of life—even
> things seemingly beyond control answer strangely to what
> is within.

The mystery, he finds, is not something functional, something to be used and manipulated. "I once cared only for images," he goes on to say, "about whose necks I could cast various 'chains of office.' . . . They were so many aldermen of the ideal, whom I wished to master the city of the soul" (*L,* 469). The poet, however, can never completely dispense with using images; in depicting the changing state of the soul the most he can do is make use of images that amalgamate in the process of conveying an intangible presence.

The condition of the soul is such that the soul will not endure its present state. It is not whole until the spirit will have outgrown human pride, until the passions will have completely overwhelmed man's bitterness and hatred, his urge to get back at the world. In *Meditations in Time of Civil War,* written four to five years after "Ego Dominus Tuus," we have a good example of the poetry of wisdom as it replaces the tangible image. The mysterious encounter with the anti-self, as described in "Ego Dominus Tuus," in this later series of poems evolves as a reflection of the self meeting with violence in the external world. Unlike "The Second Coming," written two years before, these poems have for their dominating image not a terrifying stone form which becomes animate but a stone tower which dissolves around the person of the speaker, leaving him confirmed in his solitude and assured of the redeeming power of his imagination.

There is no need to discuss at great length the pattern worked out in the seven poems composing the *Meditations;* those poems have been analyzed brilliantly by Thomas Whitaker.[8] We need only say that, throughout, the speaker is in search of an image, a form, a dream perhaps that will dispel the uncertainty of his own means of confronting reality; he wants the strength that will "but take our greatness with our violence . . . our greatness with our bitterness" (poem I). The series comes to a climax in poem VII, and we shall concentrate here primarily on that last poem.

Until poem VII two types of images exist in unresolved opposition with each other: 1) images which suggest sweetness, light, or lyrical stasis, and 2) images which point to harshness and ruin in the real world. Composite figures of transformation linking 1) and 2) (the two examples which follow are the most notable) attempt, not without irony, to build up out of images of the real world symbols of beauty and peace: a) "an acre of stony ground, / Where the symbolic rose can break in flower"; b) "O honey-bees, / Come build in the empty house of the stare." Such symbols, taking the series as a whole, collapse with the supposition that fulfilment—human or artistic—is anything more than a hope. We might ask of the speaker just what "the changeless work of art" is that he thinks is possible (poem III); or in what sense "these stones" of the tower (cf. the tower at Ballylee) will remain a "monument" to the poet (poem IV).

Poem VII suggests that keeping the imagination "responsible" to the real world depends on the effective use of "daemonic images." The first two-thirds of the poem somewhat parallel the diametric form of "The Two Trees," written thirty years before; "violent" images construed to be operative in the external world are opposed to "quiescent" images conceived by looking within. The unicorns and closed eyes of the ladies (ll. 17–26) are meant to signify an undisturbed innerworld of the imagination "when hearts are full / Of their own sweetness" and where "nothing but stillness can remain." By such images the speaker seems to have resolved his sense of bitterness and violence. Earlier (ll. 5–16) the physical landscape at night catches his inner eye with "monstrous familiar images," and he almost shouts out, like any man in the crowd, "for vengeance on the murderers of Jacques Molay" (the martyred Knight Templar recalled from fourteenth-century France). Caught up as he is in a frenzy, the speaker nonetheless exhausts that demonic urge by the enactment of a phantasmagoria. One is reminded here of Dante's prototype of the outraged, ineffectual Ugolino [9]—

> In cloud-pale rags, or in lace,
> The rage-driven, rage-tormented, and rage-hungry troop,
> Trooper belabouring trooper, biting at arm or at face,
> Plunges towards nothing, arms and fingers spreading wide
> For the embrace of nothing. . . .

The clouds which register these tumbling images, as the speaker gazes from his "tower-top" into the night, subsequently change into the medievalish unicorns which "bear ladies upon their backs." It is a kind of easeful reverie that might well follow after the earlier excitement; but "frenzies bewilder," the speaker notes, and "reveries perturb the mind." His mental conjuring evokes extraneous images—followed by the eye rather than born of visionary intensity—and as a result they succeed only in leaving the speaker unsatisfied.

No "stillness can remain," the speaker finds, no "sweetness," no "loveliness." Troopers, unicorns, ladies, all surprisingly turn to "brazen hawks." "The eyes of aquamarine" of the unicorns, the "musing eyes" of the ladies, "eyes [of the speaker?] that rage has brightened"—give place

to an "indifferent multitude," envisioned because of "the eye's compla-
cency." Nothing remains now "but grip of claw." The visual image re-
cedes with a vengeance: "clanging wings . . . have put out the moon."
And we are left with the self-consuming image of the mind itself, the
"hawk." [10]

What lies in the wake of that image? "Nor self-delighting reverie, /
Nor hate of what's to come, nor pity for what's gone." A certain tough-
ness succeeds to what Yeats in "An Acre of Grass" calls "the loose imagination." The external thing now, we feel, does not dominate. The "brazen hawks" hover between the demonic and the daimonic, a concentrated image which threateningly dispels what has preceded. It shares in
no landscape, no identifiable past. But like the sphinx of "The Second
Coming" it is perhaps redeemingly foreboding; in spite of its negative
implication it seems to have come into being from a source more provocative than a cloud. It is a fateful harbinger, startling the speaker into a
new awareness of his self-deception, "shadowing forth" like Milton's elemental powers (as the speaker in poem II observes) "how the daemonic
rage / Imagined everything."

But the "rage" has played itself out by line 32, and as a result the last
stanza of poem VII falls rather than ascends to its conclusion. The
speaker's words are those of a man relieved to find he has returned to
himself, and has not succumbed to something misallied with his nature.
The wisdom he has come by is not what those who are actively engaged
in life can "understand or share"; and he reproves his "ambitious heart"
for thinking that by having recourse to a power other than his own
imagination he might leave his mark on the world. He concludes with
this half-resigned affirmation of his faith: "the abstract joy, / The half-
read wisdom of daemonic images, / Suffice the ageing man as once the
growing boy."

A precarious kinship exists between the demonic and the spiritual,
and this is suggested in poems II and VII where the word "demonic"
was originally used by Yeats for "daemonic." The revision seems auspi-
cious, and, as in "The Second Coming" (as well as in "Meru," "The
Gyres," and "Lapis Lazuli") it appears related to the message of the
poem, which is: unless the demiurge is converted somehow by the imagination, the demonic will have sway in the world. Yeats indeed maintained that the leading poets have a vision of evil. The older he was the
more conscious he became of an unyielding energy the body wanted to
express. Age notwithstanding, the poet was obliged to train his imagina-

tion upon the insistent beating of his heart; and this, we find, made him track through his emotions more deeply into the strange and tenebrous realm of the psyche.

In poem VII of *Meditations* the speaker comes out weak but relatively clean from his struggle with reality. He has found that violence, while it is contagious, can be turned in upon itself, dissolved in the process of acting out emotional rage, keeping down, like Lear, *Hysterica Passio*. He finds there is no more than temporary escape in reverie or fantasy. The strength of the urge to revenge or destroy has to be met by a force even greater in intensity, a "daemonic rage," as Yeats has it, which does not delude the mind with subjective images; it is a power that holds its own, without having to actualize what the self—mind or body—wants, or strives or reaches out for. It is an energy that exhausts by comprehending the limitations of self, and without lulling into euphoria the mind or senses. As it will prove, the struggle against the external world is not a denial but a fulfillment of "responsibility" to the world,[11] for the very reason that it intensifies the perpetual struggle with the self for daimonic control and eventual wisdom.

The daimonic power Yeats was in search of was not authoritarian. It did demand of the individual, however, spiritual control. It was an innate power, internally directed. And if an indomitable pride goaded Yeats in that search, it was because he was only too aware that his insights were not shared by the multitude.

As Yeats learned from the Brahmin Mohini Chatterjee, and through his affiliation with the Golden Dawn Society, commitment to the transpersonal ideal of the Self is commensurate with aspiration to the godhead within (the realization of one's personal Daimon);[12] and though this aspiration would be mutual or even communal, it finally proves itself evidence of the aspirant's spiritual superiority. This indeed presented a dilemma: Yeats was confronted with his own pride in undertaking his spiritual reformation. A communicant like him could attempt to resolve the irony either by subordinating himself to an objectified concept of godhead (possibly Yeats's aim as a member of the Golden Dawn), or else by wholly expending that energy which makes him conscious of the personal self in the reformative process (this is the province of Yeats the poet).

In any case, the man intent on scaling spiritual heights does not do so without cognitional incentive from the world around him; and as a result the process seldom escapes being, or wanting to be, communicated. However little it may understand of the process, the world in its turn may unwittingly be heir to the poet's attempt at personal liberation. Yeats, at any rate, would insist that a man's spirit is never free of *Anima Mundi,* the soul of the world.

To judge the extent of Yeats's personal liberation, let us here examine the "violent annunciation" Yeats said he had in mind when he wrote "Leda and the Swan." He was prompted to write the poem, as he remarks in the famous note appended to the first two printings, "because the editor [George Russell] of a political review [*Irish Statesman*] asked me. . . . [B]ut as I wrote, bird and lady took such possession of the scene that all politics went out of it" (*P,* 828). Yeats probably had in mind writing yet another poem like *Meditations in Time of Civil War,* directly relating his own position to that of the political and physical skirmishes taking place in Ireland. Instead, what he wrote was made over, as he reveals in a letter two years later (June 1925), in the form of a "classic enunciation" (*L,* 709).

In February 1925 Yeats had completed what we know now as Book V of *A Vision,* "Dove or Swan," to which "Leda and the Swan" serves as prologue. In Book V Yeats accounts through myth for the origin of Western culture, and thus rounds out the basic concern of *A Vision*: conceptualizing as a cyclic process the spiritual history of the self. In Book V Yeats reviews the history of Western culture in terms of the contending principles of pure soul (the "dove") and the "generated soul" (the self-transforming passion of the "swan"). Like Schopenhauer, Yeats considered the forces of history as outward evidence of the psychological conflict between the physical and spiritual inclinations of the self. The swan represents "annunciation" of the classical age as a tragic division of the divine act into acts of "Love" and "War." The dove, in contrast, derives from the Judeo-Christian symbol of peace and quietude. As the epiphanic image of God the dove is a spiritual and not a violent, or sexual, symbol of the Annunciation. The values of the classical and the Christian age exist in tension with each other in Yeats's philosophy of history; and because of this we may say that "Leda and the Swan," while describing a pre-Christian event, originates "psychopoetically" from a retrospective awareness of Christian values.

Psychopoesis may be defined as a revelatory conjunction of ideas, images, or feelings that have been a long time gestating and which at some compelling moment enables the poet to realize in artistic form an otherwise unrelievable tension, or state of mind. Through the ordering energy of the psychopoetic imagination seemingly disparate images are illuminated by some common matrix of expression—what Yeats means, perhaps, by referring to "Leda" as a "classic enunciation."

In "Leda and the Swan" the matrix, a traditional myth, takes on dimension by its disguised immediacy, what we may assume to be for Yeats its psychological implications. Taken as an imaginative event, the poem and the physical or natural energies which it describes, not only emerge from, but in the end find expression as, an act of mind. A complex of contrary forces—reflections upon the human and superhuman, the male and the female, the bestial and the beautiful, passion and passiveness, sexual energy and historical violence—once enmeshed with each other culminate in a moment of illumination: a revelation darkly shared, brought home in the form of a question.[13]

Analysis of the psychopoetic content of "Leda" makes one aware both of the interpenetrating imagery and ambiguous syntax in the poem and of correlative images and associations found elsewhere in Yeats's writing—the most revealing being those in Yeats's account of his spiritual marriage with Maud Gonne.

The poem therefore, as I read it, is to be approached on two levels, by closely explicating the text and by following through a pattern of extra-textual associations. Seen as a psychopoetic unit the poetic lines and images seem increasingly fluid, and separate images (girl, swan, wall, tower) appear to converge upon a common psychological ground. Like "The Second Coming," where images of human violence are subsumed by the composite image of a millennial beast, in "Leda and the Swan" images of violence, sexual and historical, are meant to be absorbed by the apparent unity of a superhuman consciousness—a daimonic intelligence which transcends those very events it initiates through its animalistic (or human) need for physical incarnation.

"Leda and the Swan" is undoubtedly the best example of that delight Yeats said he had "in all that displayed great problems through sensuous images" (*M,* 343). The problem which concerns us—if we may recapitulate the poet's spiritual development—originated with the interposition between lover and immortal beloved (Yeats's image of Maud Gonne) of the sensuous image the poet first identified with his sometime mistress, Olivia Shakespear. It may be more correct to say that the supersensual image of the immortal beloved at the time prevented full realization of any sensuous image. The aftermath of his spiritual and his sexual passion consequently resulted in the lover's falling out with both his inamorata.

In "Leda and the Swan" (1923) the lover makes his startling appearance as a god, and here in a most striking way the sensuous and the spiritual images are momently conjoined. The person of the godhead is envisioned as being consumed with animal passion, until his "brute blood" is apotheosized once again as spiritual energy. And Leda the mortal is left the undecided beneficiary or victim of that fervid visitation.

One might say a miraculous change has taken place in Yeats's conception of poetry: it is as if (to use words the poet used later in "Hound Voice") images had suddenly "waken[ed] in the blood" to tear off the constrictive veil of the physical world. The poem seems to represent an instinctive fusion of body and mind, and to promise possible reparation of the spiritual breach between woman and man, man and God, world and self—joinable opposites which, as Jung claimed, may contribute finally to the reintegration of the human psyche.

Like other of Yeats's memorable poems—"The Wild Swans at Coole," "The Second Coming," "Byzantium"—"Leda and the Swan" has a highly distinctive poetic form. It is preeminent among the modern poems based on the Leda myth (Rilke, D. H. Lawrence, Hilda Doolittle, T. Sturge Moore, Oliver Gogarty, Aldous Huxley, May Sarton all wrote poems about Leda) in that it is a masterpiece of compression. The poem bears comparison especially with the plastic arts in that it attempts through words a fusion or interplay of sensibility that no conventional image can convey. Critics in search of a specific source for the poem will continue to be puzzled by the number of paintings and sculptural versions of the Leda myth, constituting as Charles Madge says "two main traditional representations . . . in one of which she is recumbent and acquiescent, while in the other she is standing and is being taken by force."[14] Our analysis suggests a solution to the quest for pictorial sources by regarding the poem as a composite action, picturing through its sequence of imaginal and verbal ambiguities both the aggressive and the passive instincts of girl and swan.[15]

We may begin the explication of "Leda" by noting in "Leda and the Swan" the reflexive opposition of concrete and abstract imagery.[16] Leda, "the staggering girl," is identified through concrete detail: "Her thighs," "her nape," "her helpless breast," "her loosening thighs." The swan, on the other hand, is never referred to in the poem itself as a "swan." He is described as an overpowering abstraction—"the great wings," "the dark webs," "that white rush," "the brute blood," "the indifferent beak." It may be the purely mechanical simplicity of the grammar that finally requires pronominal identification of the "swan," in the third, fourth, and thirteenth lines of the poem. But at these points the use of pronouns tends to humanize the essential action. The relationship of swan and girl is not only the relationship of god to mortal but of male to female, the notion of divinity momentarily converted into something human, albeit animalistically derived:

[3]   her nape caught in his bill,
[4]   He holds her helpless breast upon his breast.

[13] Did she put on his knowledge with his power
[14] Before the indifferent beak could let her drop?

In these last lines of the poem (13 and 14) we are reminded once again of the original separation between the personal and the divine, and the distinction between animal and spiritual energy.

What then about the intervening lines, 5 to 12, in which the climax of the sexual act is quite unforgettably described? In these lines there is not only a conspicuous absence of pronominal forms (only one pronominal phrase is used, "her loosening thighs") but more importantly the distinction between the concrete (or personal) and the abstract gives way to a profound ambiguity—the more astonishing because it is fully sustained throughout the second quatrain and for the first two lines of the sestet.

The middle section of the poem is best approached by returning briefly to the opening quatrain. Essentially what we find in the poem is a complex reversal of roles, and this is anticipated first by the phrase in line 2, "the staggering girl." Here the immediate meaning requires that the participle be regarded as intransitive (that is, the girl is literally staggering; the action is physical, concrete); but a possible, secondary meaning suggests the transitive form of the verb, making the swan, not the girl, the object that is affected (that is, the girl "staggers" the mind, imagination or willpower of the swan-god; the action takes on figurative meaning). The undercurrent meaning thus moves in a direction contrary to the direction of the apparent meaning, and makes the situation as described bilateral, with agent and recipient of the "action" potentially interchangeable. R. P. Blackmur explains this kind of interchange in "Leda" by citing Yeats's much-quoted doctrine of the unitive imagination. The doctrine would here apply to our organic perception of the poetic "action" in "Leda" rather than to the action of figures described in the poem: "That the borders of our mind are ever shifting, and that many minds can flow into one another, as it were, and create or reveal a single mind, a single energy. . . . That this great mind can be evoked by symbols" (*E,* 28). Commenting on the application of Yeat's words, Blackmur observes: "Copulation is the obvious nexus for spiritual as well as physical seed." [17] Perception of a unity in the poem thus tends to break down the separation between elements constituting the tension, or dichotomies, in the poem.

A second example of the ambiguous play of current and undercurrent meaning in "Leda" occurs in line 4. The possibility here is perhaps harder to grasp.

> He holds her helpless breast upon his breast.

The ambiguity arises from the provocative omission of internal punctuation. A semi-colon and two commas mark the caesura at the end of the second foot, the third foot, and the second foot, in lines 1 to 3 respectively. The reader is left in line 4 with an option as to where to pause, if he is inclined to pause at all. The line as written above follows through on the 2, 3, 2 caesural pattern previously established if we pause briefly after "helpless breast." But what if we mentally punctuate the line as follows:

> He holds her, helpless, breast upon his breast.

This reading possibly reverses the primary sense of the line. "Helpless" can be taken to modify "he" as well as "her." Our initial impression of the violence of the swan thus is countered by the suggestion of a quite different form of intimacy: the swan, "helpless," would seem to be arrested by his willful embrace of Leda.

No regular metrical pattern is to be found in "Leda and the Swan," but there is a pervading rhythmic base in which verbal stress displaces the accent-guided line. In the first quatrain one finds a counterbalancing of verbal and rhythmic movement. The rhythm pushes the action forward, while the words tend to hold back, delay the action. Lines 1 and 2 are run-on, indicating by linear separation a reluctance of the opposed images to merge, a reluctance which by line 3 is gradually relaxed:

[1]   . . . the great wings beating still
[2] Above the staggering girl, her thighs caressed
[3] By the dark webs. . . .

The counterpoint is furthered by the connotation of individual words. Most conspicuous is the word "still." As a form of enantiosis, coming at a pivotal point in the verse line, "still" implies both continuity and fixity. It is as if, as Leo Spitzer suggests, the great wings have never stopped beating as a mythic event.[18] And yet the bird is described as having just dropped down upon the unsuspecting Leda. He is pictured balanced on her thighs, in movement and yet without moving, as he beats the air with his wings. Taken this way the image conveys a feeling of vibrant and timeless stasis. And in this connection the word "caught" in line 3 and the word "holds" in line 4 both serve to reinforce our impression of dynamic stillness.

Consider again line 4 in juxtaposition with the preceding clause in line three:

[3]   her nape caught in his bill
[4] He holds her helpless breast upon his breast.

To which of the two figures does the word "caught" apply? One's immediate response would be to regard the swan as having done the catching ("caught" read as a past participle). Presumably he is the agent. Considering the ambiguous syntax of line 4, however, line 3 may be read with reverse meaning: the girl may be construed as struggling in such a way as to have forced "her nape" into "his bill" ("caught" read as past tense), making *him* "helpless" even though "he holds her." This reversal of the apparent meaning suggests that Leda's role may be actively rather than passively submissive. As John F. Adams puts it: "While Leda— woman—is violated, in spite of herself her own passion draws her into a participation in the experience."[19] It is possible then to regard the swan not as clutching Leda in a vise of brute strength but as coupling with her in mutual embrace.

Are these speculations about lines 3 and 4 at all borne out by the central section of the poem? Our approach will be facilitated by asking from this point on: Who of the two principals is acting and who is being acted upon? Consider first the opening of the second quatrain:

How can those terrified vague fingers push
The feathered glory from her loosening thighs?

Whose fingers are doing the pushing? It would seem most obvious that Leda's are. She is the one who appears "terrified." But is she? And how do we account for the fact that her fingers are "vague"? They are "vague" in the sense that they are "wandering" (from the Latin root), but this suggests that she is not pushing to get rid of the terror the swan inspires in her.

Yet the swan may also be regarded as having the "vague fingers." The dark webs or the great wings terminate in what only imperfectly resemble "fingers." And this approximation is expressed by the word "vague." But then why should the swan be "terrified"? That word was once used to denote a sense of being irritated, tormented, teased.[20] If this meaning is permitted, then we may make out the swan to be a creature who must vent his frustration, satisfy some natural longing. The girl, in turn, may be regarded as the innocent victim, or as the source for alleviation of an intolerable abstinence

If we consider the ambiguity of the action being described in line 5, we get some idea of the interchangeability of the emotion being expressed, and we can begin to appreciate better the psychological complexity which inheres in the sexual drama. Take now lines 5 and 6 together:

> How can those terrified vague fingers push
> The feathered glory from her loosening thighs?

This statement may be read at least four ways. How can Leda ever get free of the swan? How can Leda hope or even want to get free of the swan? How can the "terrified" swan, frustrated in accomplishing his will, succeed in begetting offspring (his "feathered glory") through Leda? And finally, how can Leda succeed in begetting issue worthy of the swan's natural or supernatural resplendence? The question in the poem is so phrased that we cannot tell apart the anxiety and the desire of girl and swan. The reading of the lines depends upon whom we take to be the subject of the statement, upon the kind of emphasis we place on the words "can" and "push," and thirdly upon how we interpret the phrase "feathered glory."

Consider in this context the last two lines of the quatrain:

> [7] And how can body, laid in that white rush,
> [8] But feel the strange heart beating where it lies?

Another question, and again a complementarity of meaning. The sense of struggle, urgency, or anxiety—however one may read it—implied in lines 5 and 6 is weakened rather than reinforced by lines 7 and 8. Here the ambiguity is substantially reduced, and even though it is still possible to posit a double meaning for the statement, the question implies a fusion of sensibility in relation to the experience of swan and girl. If the narrator is here speaking from the point of view of the swan the question would read as follows: How can the physical body, *her* body, exposed to this gathering of energy, but feel its imminent release giving life to her and me—as though her heart were mine and mine hers? And from the point of view of Leda the question posed would be: How can the physical body, *my* body, ravished, but feel the expended force of his will, and so transform my sense of being that I feel *his* heart? (It is quite immaterial whether the ambiguous "it" in line 8 refers to "body" or "heart"; whatever the reference, the interchange of meaning in this case signifies a mutual transformation through sexual embrace.) The lines imply that the sense of separation is what brings anxiety and induces struggle, and that such a feeling of separation can be ameliorated in sexual climax. The breaking of sexual tension described in the lines that follow (9 to 11) does not necessarily reveal portents of disaster; it can as well represent release from the feeling of fear or alienation, on the one hand, or relief from insatiable desire on the other.

In these lines (9 to 11) of the sestet describing what may be called "the ejaculation scene" one finds the ambiguity of the poem most striking:

> A shudder in the loins engenders there
> The broken wall, the burning roof and tower
> And Agamemnon dead.

"Engenders" where? we may ask. In the house of Priam or in the house of Atreus? In the womb of Leda? In the supernal consciousness of the swan? In the consciousness of a given culture? Perhaps none of these possibilities need be excluded.

What we have basically is a confrontation of the physical and the mental event. The speaker imaginatively participates in and yet obviously stands outside the situation. He witnesses Leda's rape as he would the tragedy at Troy and Argos, and understands how one event is implied in the other. From whose point of view does the speaker witness the sequel of Leda's rape? Is one partner or the other responsible

for the epic situation at Troy? By the last two lines, certainly, the whole
burden of the poem rests upon the disparity between the point of view
of Leda and the point of view of the swan: "Did she put on his knowledge with his power . . .?"

How is the physical event then—the sexual-historical relationship—to
be regarded? Is there another way of looking at the ejaculation scene
without having to fall back on a recapitulation of the historical irony?
Can that scene somehow explain the myth as an illusion of the power
expended in the sexual act? And this leads to our final correlation between textual and subtextual meaning. If the poem focuses intently on
the rape of Leda, then the line and a half describing the subsequent fall
of Troy and of the house of Atreus is in no sense a digression. The
unity of the poem is not disrupted if we regard the mytho-historical reference in lines 10 and 11 at the same time as sexual imagery. The "broken wall" reminds us of the walls of Troy, but then again it rings up associations with "maidenhead" and "womb." The "burning roof and
tower" reinforce our picture of Troy being destroyed, but then too it
may suggest the burning effect following sexual climax.[21] The swan's
experience and knowledge is the kind which exempts him from further
involvement in this fatal course of events at Troy. His wisdom replen-
ished after the rape of Leda, he assumes again the indifference of a god.
The implication, once more, is that the historical scene represents nothing but an extension of the willful violence that may be dissolved in the
sexual act.[22]

And with this we conclude our formal exegesis. We may turn now
to examine the sources of Yeats's images of the "tower" and the "wall,"
trying to establish in what way these images are related to the psychopoetic content of the poem.

Giorgio Melchiori mentions significantly that in line 11 of the first
draft of "Leda and the Swan" the word "Tower" is capitalized, "though
its symbolic value in the context is not immediately apparent.[23] Yeats
himself thought of the tower he had renovated in Ballylee as a "permanent symbol of my work plainly visible to the passer-by." [24] And all
those who have dealt with the symbol in Yeats's work have, to use Virginia Moore's words, taken it to mean "the pursuit of wisdom; and wisdom meant a reconciliation of myriads of opposites." [25] Yeats himself,
an ardent member of the Golden Dawn Society, had probably aspired to

the fourth level of initiation and therefore, we may suppose, was baptized symbolically *Pharos Illuminans,* "Illuminating Tower of Light." [26] Furthermore, as T. R. Henn points out,[27] Yeats was no doubt familiar with one of the symbolistic cards of the Tarot pack, "The Lightning Struck Tower," an image which foreshadowed for him the violence and disintegration that beset Ireland in its time of troubles and that potentially posed a threat to Yeats's tower at Ballylee. Finally, the symbol of the "broken" tower is used in the poem "The Tower" and in the series of seven poems, *Meditations in Time of Civil War.*[28] Given this range of associations we have to ascertain how the tower image in "Leda" comes to be a phallic symbol, "phallos" as well as "pharos."

We may begin our investigation by quoting a passage from an earlier poem, "The Tower," with an eye to establishing that the tower initially may have represented a sublimation, or displacement, of sexual impulse.[29] The passage I have in mind is a critical moment in that poem. Let us review briefly what leads up to it. The speaker has complained bitterly about his "decrepit age" and finds that because he once had "excited, passionate, fantastical / Imagination . . . / That . . . expected the impossible," he is confronted now with two alternatives: either to "be content with argument and deal / In abstract things; or be derided by / A sort of battered kettle at the heel." In these lines the narrator restates the problem his entire life as a poet has posed; he is caught in a perpetually unresolved vacillation between the abstractions of the soul and an agonizing self-consciousness. That is the argumentative setting. The psychopoetic setting is as follows: "I pace upon the battlements [of the tower] and stare / On the foundations of a house [the house of Mary Hynes, see below] . . . / And send imagination forth / Under the day's declining beam, and call / Images and memories / From ruin . . . / For I would ask a question of them all" (*P,* 410–11). The poet claims for the imagination the power to dredge the past and exercise control over what may unconsciously have impressed itself on the mind. What follows in "The Tower" is a mixture of historical and imaginative recall, a blend of associations of the physical environs of the tower with images of his own creating. He questions what each of these associations and images means before dismissing them, but is anxious about letting go one early creation of his, the wild and passionate Red Hanrahan. And this is the passage that I suggest helps us better understand the tower image.

leave Hanrahan,
For I need all his mighty memories.

Old lecher with a love on every wind,
Bring up out of that deep considering mind
All that you have discovered in the grave,
For it is certain that you have
Reckoned up every unforeknown, unseeing
Plunge, lured by a softening eye,
Or by a touch or a sigh,
Into the labyrinth of another's being;

Does the imagination dwell the most
Upon a woman won or a woman lost?
If on the lost, admit you turned aside
From a great labyrinth out of pride,
Cowardice, some silly over-subtle thought. . . .

Is it any wonder, in view of this tormented questioning, that four months after the publication of this poem the author should make the statement to Olivia Shakespear that "only two topics can be of the least interest to a serious and studious mind—sex and the dead" (*L,* 730)? In the Hanrahan passage of "The Tower" the speaker is summoning from the grave a thwarted, perpetually unsated creature of the imagination. The interrogation is in the form of self-reproof for spiritual and intellectual pride; for all his lofty imaginings about the ideal woman the speaker is left in the throes of a subterranean agony. The figure of the speaker pacing on the battlements of his tower becomes an ironic foil to the speaker later summoning up from the sexual, psychological, and terrestrial deep images that want to become conscious elements of the imagination.[30] And to be sure, it is from the time of this poem, "The Tower," that we can date the inception of Yeats's frankly sexual love poetry.

It is as though the tower is a pivotal image, an image of transformation, its recall progressively removing the speaker from his spiritual height to the unexpressed recesses of the human psyche. In this light we can understand the implications of Yeats's abundant correspondence with Olivia Shakespear in the fall of 1916. She is the person to whom, for the first time in his letters, he makes mention of the tower he has recently contracted to buy:

I hear there is quite a sound cottage at the foot of my castle, so I may be there even before the castle is roofed (*L,* 615).

Subsequent reference to the peasant's cottage juxtaposed with the noble, staunch tower carried with it symbolic overtones. And though the meaning of the tower and the peasant cottage as symbols of pride and humility have been alluded to by Yeats's biographers, its psychopoetic associations have not been fully explored.

Having in mind the analysis just applied to the Hanrahan passage in "The Tower," one wonders about this seemingly casual remark of Yeats in a letter written October 27, 1927 to Mrs. Shakespear:

> I send you a couple of Ballylee pictures—one my bed and one of the Tower from the river side. (*L*, 730)

The juxtaposition here of bed, tower, and water is unavoidably suggestive, though it is difficult to say whether Yeats actually intended any sexual overtones. But the correspondence with Mrs. Shakespear is undeniably forthright in the letter dated May 25, 1926. Although the entire letter is relevant, I quote here just the opening paragraph:

> My dear Olivia: We are at our Tower and I am writing poetry as I always do here, and as always happens, no matter how I begin, it becomes love poetry before I am finished with it. I have lots of subjects in my head including a play about Christ meeting the worshippers of Dionysus on the mountain side—no doubt that will somehow become love poetry too. I have brought but two books, Baudelaire and MacKenna's *Plotinus*. Plotinus is a most ardent and wonderful person. I am also writing answers to a long series of questions sent me by a reader of *A Vision*, and Plotinus helps me there. Do you remember the story of Buddha who gave a flower to some one, who in his turn gave another a silent gift and so from man to man for centuries passed on the doctrine of the Zen school? One feels at moments as if one could with a touch convey a vision—that the mystic way and sexual love use the same means—opposed yet parallel existences. (*L*, 714-15)

This passage shows Yeats, like Carl Jung, his contemporary in Böllingen, adept at rooting the tower—as an archetype of psychological transformation—in the earth. For Yeats it was "an image of mysterious wisdom won by toil," as he says in "The Phases of the Moon," and symbolizes a knowledge that is at once sexual and spiritual.

Complementary to Yeats's concern with "the mystic way and sexual love" was his preoccupation with "the dead." A statement Yeats makes in a letter to Sturge Moore, dated April 17, 1929, comes to mind and we shall use it as a proposition for the argument which follows. "Sexual desire dies," Yeats declares, "because every touch consumes the Myth and yet the Myth that cannot be so consumed becomes a spectre" (*YM,* 154). We shall proceed now by traveling over trodden ground to see if we can find the specter causing Yeats to write "Leda and the Swan."

Giorgio Melchiori reminds us that the lecture on "The Irish Dramatic Movement," which Yeats delivered when he went to Stockholm in December 1923 to receive the Nobel prize, "was necessarily prepared at a time when Yeats had just drafted his sonnet 'Leda and the Swan.'" And he goes on to quote a passage in that lecture that strikes up interesting associations.

> I have in Galway a little old tower, and when I climb to the top of it I can see at no great distance a green field where stood once the thatched cottage of a famous country beauty, the mistress of a small local landed proprietor. I have spoken to old men and women who remembered her, though all are dead now, and they spoke of her as the old men upon the walls of Troy spoke of Helen.[31]

Yeats points with considerable pride to a girl in Ireland who might be Helen's equal. And it is possible that Yeats was drawing for himself a parallel between the "little old tower"—actually one of the most imposing Norman towers in Ireland—and the "little old foundation" of the house where the girl Mary Hynes lived, described in an essay published first in 1899 (*M,* 22). That essay, which we shall turn to presently, Yeats may possibly have reread in preparing the Stockholm address. It bears on the first page a footnote that he added in 1924 while editing the work for reissue in 1925: on recalling the story of the famous beauty of Ballylee he makes a point of announcing to the reader that the tower "is now my property" (*M,* 22).

Mary Hynes is the "country beauty" whom the bard of Galway, Anthony Raftery, celebrated in verse, but otherwise it seems got little satisfaction from.[32] She lived at Ballylee, a very small neighborhood in County Galway; and the neighborhood became famous perhaps less because of her than because Raftery wrote about her.

As Norman Jeffares points out,[33] it was most likely that Yeats (who had poor eyesight) should have identified himself with the blind bard Raftery and that he should have identified with Mary Hynes his own immortal love, Maud Gonne.

Only seven or eight months removed from his first "spiritual marriage" with Maud Gonne, Yeats sat down to write about the seventy-year old story of Raftery and Mary Hynes: it was the essay published in 1899, symbolically entitled "Dust hath closed Helen's eye." Mary Hynes, Yeats tells us, was reputed to have had as many as a dozen suitors call on her the same day, and her beauty caused the death of at least two. She herself died young "because the gods loved her" (*M*, 28). In that early essay Mary is compared for the first time to the fatal heroine of Troy, who somehow made "the old men of Troy" grow "gentle" when "she passed by on the walls" (*M*, 28).

Helen, we should remember, by 1908 becomes identified in Yeats's poetry with Maud Gonne. Maud's fall from favor in Ireland was lamented, and at the same time celebrated, by the poet, becoming his first and foremost example of "tragic defeat." However, in the same paragraph of that letter of April 27, 1929 to Sturge Moore, declaring sexual desire to be a myth, Yeats significantly mentions that he "used to puzzle Maud Gonne by always avowing ultimate defeat as a test." He implied by this that the Valkyrie-like maiden, whose sense of history made her put a premium upon violence as the way to liberate Ireland, still had something to learn about life. The defeat of personal hopes and ambitions to Yeats's mind was the principal means of enjoining upon the proud heart spiritual humility. In the nineties Yeats had begun thinking of himself as Maud's mentor, and by 1908, when he initiated the "Helen poems," and agreed to a second "spiritual marriage" with Maud, he had come to think of her as "my child more than my sweet-heart." She is my innocence and I her wisdom," he declared (January 21, 1909).[34] "How much of the best I have done and still do is but the attempt to explain myself to her? If she understood I should lack a reason for writing" (January 22, 1909).[35]

The largely unpublished diaries of 1908 and 1909 strongly suggest that Yeats's spiritual marriage was the background and psychological excuse for the writing of "Leda and the Swan." And in considering this matter it is well to sum up what we have determined thus far in regard to the mythic constituents of Yeats's image of Maud Gonne. What we have is a triangular relationship, best explained by a second passage from "The Tower." In that poem the story of Mary Hynes is reviewed for the third and last time in Yeats's work. The speaker in the poem has just finished telling of a song Raftery made of Mary Hynes:

> Strange, but the man who made the song was blind;
> Yet, now I have considered it, I find

> That nothing strange; the tragedy began
> With Homer that was a blind man,
> And Helen has all living hearts betrayed.

The speaker, the bard Raftery, and Homer are regarded as having been bound together in tragic union with their fatal Helen.

We then begin to see how Yeats traces all this back to the myth of Leda, who after all begot Helen, and who, by 1926, is identified by the poet with Maud Gonne (the "Ledaean body" of "Among School Children"). It is as though the ambiguity of the question about Leda at the end of "Leda and the Swan" reflects the poet's once hopeful and then ironic attitude to the stalwart innocence of the woman he had celebrated as a modern Helen. Because his relationship with Maud Gonne remained unconsummated, the poet's imagination fastened quite decidedly in his later years on the themes of sex and death. Is it possible he thought he could trace back and resolve by use of the myth his continuing psychological involvement with the woman he had so religiously loved?

Let us not underestimate Yeats's dealings with the dead. He was interested in spiritualistic phenomena not because he believed in ghosts, but because he could escape neither his instincts nor his need to be in touch with *Anima Mundi,* the soul of the world. After all, ever since he began writing the essays *Ideas of Good and Evil* (1895–1903)—and especially since he began writing his autobiography (1909), which led eventually to inditement of *A Vision* (1925)—Yeats was concerned with tracing his heritage back in time. This enabled him to determine his psychological lineage with respect to great artists, from Blake and Shakespeare to Sophocles and Homer; and it allowed him to deal with psychological problems in terms of some formal archetype. The procedure would give dignity and heroic value to his constant struggle to understand himself and, in a larger sense, to understand the psychological dynamic of the daimonic or transpersonal Self.

Both Yeats and Maud Gonne were members in the Hermetic Order of the Golden Dawn, they both attended seances, and they also "communed" spiritually with each other. But they were too sophisticated to believe their spiritualistic probings proved anything but their own spiritual needs; and when they entered into their second spiritual marriage in 1908 (Maud fervently, perhaps desperately, and Yeats willingly, though skeptical), they were each exploring their capacity for love. We have Virginia Moore's testimony as to Maud's admission when she was an old woman that she loved Yeats, but not in any physical sense; [36] and we have all the proof of Yeats's later years that he must have believed, though he may not have been completely aware of it, that his spiritual love for Maud could never be consummated except *through* sexual union, that the "mystic way and sexual love" are inextricably related.

It was his and Maud's spiritual pride no less than his own intellectual pride that had to be broken, for Yeats to come to a more complete understanding of his transpersonal Self. That this might be accomplished, the myth of sexual desire had to run its course, and so be thoroughly consumed.

Here we can profitably return to the matter of Yeats's and Maud's spiritual marriage and see how it may possibly have shaped its imaginative, more vigorous counterpart in "Leda and the Swan." We may piece together our argument from the information and excerpts that Virginia Moore provides in her examination of Yeats's diaries of 1908 and 1909. Miss Moore's principal source is the "large white calf-skin notebook" formerly in Mrs. Yeats's possession.[37]

The spiritual marriage between Yeats and Maud Gonne begins in their attempt to achieve inseparable union by an exchange of psychic identities (or masks). This necessitated the obliteration of their personal identities. "She made me and I her," is how Yeats described it in January 1909. The marriage was based on a communication through dream correspondence and astral vision (controlled release of spiritual tension). Throughout, however, their attempt to sustain their sense of union was being undermined by the intrusion of physical elements and by the circumstances of waking life. Miss Moore notes three instances of this which are pertinent to our correlation of the marriage with the sexual event described in "Leda and the Swan": 1) The first week in August 1908 Yeats saw Maud's face beautifully but palely transfigured and himself weakly joined with her by a "sort of phantom ecstasy." This was accompanied by his impression of a swan floating in water ("sensual emotion dreams of water"—*A,* 330) and a figure in white that, as Miss Moore paraphrases it, "seemed to pass through the room." This was followed by a dream in which Maud reproached Yeats because she could not break down some barrier. 2) On October 20 Maud herself records in Yeats's journal that she and Yeats "became one being with an ecstasy I cannot describe." Then Yeats appeared to her in a dream "very beautiful and happy and triumphant"; but she was awakened from this dream-state by "a great gust of wind blowing through the room," and by the accompanying voice of an archangel who announced that from her union a "great beauty may be born," once she has been "purified by suffering." 3) Three months before, on July 26, Maud had written to Yeats in great excitement that "we melted into one another till we formed only *one being, a being greater than ourselves,* who felt all and knew all with double intensity." And she woke up from this dream feeling "as if life was being drawn away" from within her chest "with almost physical pain." [38]

Judging from these three examples, we may suggest that Maud's union with Yeats derived from her desire to transcend her physical being via an experience startlingly similar to immaculate conception. Yeats reports on June 20, at the very start of the marriage: "it is to be a bond of the spirit only and she lives from now on, she said, for that and her children" [Iseult and Sean]. Yeats is consciously trying to suppress any physical desire in the hope that he will be purged of it by spiritual union. The floating swan and "phantom ecstasy" conceived by him alone in his room make for a pallid exercise of the spiritual imagination when compared to the magisterial force of the picture he creates in 1923—of the swan swooping down on Leda, dissipating his animal energy in her womb. We might even imagine Yeats's description of the rape of Leda, in line 1 of the poem, as a poetic compensation for Maud's reported description of "a great gust of wind blowing through the room." If she is his innocence, as he says, and he her wisdom, then through her he should eventually be able to make known his suppressed desire.

But this attitude of Yeats was still to be a long time in developing. In 1909 the poet could only interpret his sexual longing as the betrayal of his Helen, and not as Helen's betrayal of him. While he was forming his liaison that year with a woman in London (the "harlot" that hauntingly appears in the poem "Presences"—1917) he finds himself "in continual terror of some entanglement parting" himself and Maud.

How ironic this statement is in the light of "Leda and the Swan." The "terror" he feels has yet to make itself felt in a more vital way. It is no wonder then, contrary to Miss Moore's surprise, that in 1909 Yeats should have begun thinking of Maud as his "mystic victim." If his beloved wants to pursue her spiritual correspondence with him then he must take the other road and follow out his sexual desire, even if that should mean finally separating from Maud.

This apparently is how Yeats interpreted the symbol of the inverted sword (an image which occurred to Maud before the spiritual marriage and which later in the marriage served a ritual function). Quite rightly,

Maud felt the sword meant "necessary suffering" for her (to use Miss Moore's words), spiritual purification through abstinence. Yeats, on the other hand, who in January noticed that "the old dread of physical love has [re-]awakened in her" took the sword to mean (again using Miss Moore's words) an "obligatory separation from things external." Given Yeats's dilemma, the sword appears to have been the two-edged symbol of love and death, representing frustration or else fulfillment of sexual power as a means of spiritual enlightenment. Representing the latter, the sword would point the way, paradoxically, for avoiding physical violence or vengeful destruction.

If only Maud could understand. Again, how ironic is the ecstatic proposal with which she first greeted Yeats on June 26: "If we are only strong enough to hold the door open, I think we shall obtain knowledge of life we have never dreamed of." She meant by this a life of utter purity. And this was the unwitting sting in the flesh. What Yeats wanted above all from his most intimate "friend" was to be accepted for both "good and evil." He knew there was an urge in him that could be destructive, destructive of love and soul both. And it had to be expressed if it was not going to warp his entire being. Is it any wonder that he showed his commitment to the ideal of self-enlightenment by taking for his mystic title in the Golden Dawn society: "D.E.D.I"—"Demon est Deus Inversus"? The god in man cannot be taken apart from the demon in him. The mystical marriage is necessarily a mutual expression of the demiurge, and not merely of the pure and the beautiful. It would seem to follow then that, given Maud's persistent innocence, Yeats had to fulfill himself alone.

Maud, as she once promised her father, gave herself wholly to Ireland. Not Yeats. She wanted Yeats (as she wanted also Tagore) for Ireland's sake. And Yeats wanted her; he wanted to write for her sake. But she was too strong-minded not to have her way. "You remember how, for the sake of Ireland," she said, "I hated you in politics. . . . I always felt it . . . cheated Ireland of a greater gift." That gift was his writing. But Yeats would use his writing for something better than the glorious end Maud desired. He could never give all his heart to Ireland so long as it provided only a narrow home for the soul. How beautiful and how terrible was that fiery woman who thought little enough of violence to use it as a means for gaining Ireland her independence. Clearly Maud's way was the opposite of the poet's. Yeats would take issue with the world and make love not war the test of a man's strength. It was therefore quite like Yeats that he should have found cause (from "the editor of a political review") to write a poem in which "bird and lady took such possession of the scene that all politics went out of it."

The inner scene was what Yeats concentrated on. Insofar as he was "of Ireland" he demonstrated his responsibility to that country as a metapolitician. His ability to dramatize the struggle within was his forte, and he was destined to prove the strength of his belief through his power of imagination.

In this context we may consider, once again, the psychopoetic source of the ejaculation scene in "Leda." We have tried to prepare the way for reading the mytho-historical allusions in that central passage in terms of the underlying sexual imagery. Our argument leads us to conclude not only that the physical event (the Trojan war) has its pregenital equivalent in sexual love, but that physical violence may be contained by opening the floodgates of the sexual imagination. If we consider again the circumstances attending Yeats's spiritual marriage with Maud Gonne, we can see how the espousal of spiritual purity only constrains the psyche and throws open the door to images of violence, if not to violence itself. For Yeats, of course, poetry saved the day, and he was fortunate for having the strenuousness of his work as a source of release.

The immediate aftermath of his spiritual marriage, however, was hardly so propitious. Miss Moore reports that in late January 1909 "Yeats dreamed that, walking along a path by a broken wall and precipice, he felt dizzy and longed to throw himself over." And then "from sheer horror of the Abyss," to revert to Yeats's words, the poet proceeded to suppress completely any earthy desire—in the hope of finding the redeeming "wisdom of love." He was beginning to think that it might be "my intellectual side" that is causing the barrier between himself and Maud. Yeats could not help being what he was, introspective and a visionary, while Maud the political revolutionary was an extroverted idealist. But surely there was something in that "broken wall" he dreamed about that, though it frightened him, yet offered him relief from his constraint. It may be that he would have to come down from his intellectual tower and take the same "unseeing plunge" that, as the speaker in "The Tower" infers, made Red Hanrahan eminently knowledgeable. The plunge into the Abyss would be the way down, a kind of bodily death, necessary to any subsequent spiritual ascent or wisdom. What Yeats is after, as we have already suggested, is the welcome release of psychic energy which would complement the broken wall with the burning tower (read for "wall" and "tower" their sexual equivalents). That release would end in the toppling not only of spiritual but of intellectual pride, using the only complementary means available: sexual energy. The ejaculation scene in "Leda" to be sure links the expression of sexual with the expression of imaginative energy. And had the complexity of his problem not been expressed in writing (for it would never be resolved) that desire for expression might possibly have taken effect in a more devastating way.

Miss Moore adduces evidence of Yeats's ordeal from the new diary he had begun in December 1908, apparently to contain what did not seem proper for his abortive marriage journal: an independent investigation of his spiritual impurity, the self-analysis which begins his cultural-autobiographical writings, culminating in 1925 with the transpersonal wisdom of *A Vision*. Mother Ireland, who once produced "the bravest soldiers and the most beautiful women" (*A*, 312) has become subject to the sterility of argument, warfare, hatred—so much so that the strain Yeats felt himself exposed to made him "almost hit a woman" (Miss Moore's words). "The feeling is always the same," as Yeats goes on to say: "a consciousness of energy, of certainty, and a transforming power stopped by a wall." [39] He was speaking for himself and for Ireland both. The impasse results in no small way when "a part of [a woman's] flesh becomes stone," because she is concerned with " 'something other than human life' " (*A*, 341). Commenting on his own example no less than Ireland's he could attribute "sexual abstinence, so common among young men and women in Ireland," to "hatred as a basis of imagination" (*A*, 330). It is not hard to see why Yeats's virginal profusions addressed to the Rose of all Ireland (in the volume *The Rose*) should have spawned also an apocalyptic desire to be rid of the rest of mankind. It is only after middle age that he, like Joyce writing at this same time, begins to understand and express his bitterness and reveal how it originates in the sacred reproof of the flesh.

The spiritual imagination is not holy until it fully taps the primordial reserves of human passion. The discipline that Yeats doggedly insists upon in the published section of his diary for 1909 is not really possible without his being made to surrender the old spiritual ideal, the realization of a discarnate beauty that presumably was to culminate his relationship with Maud Gonne.

In the spring of 1909 Yeats was told by an astrologer he would "soon receive a violent shock and . . . lose something," something that would enable him to "find himself." He had in part anticipated this strange announcement when he reconciled himself for his loss of Maud: hoping "that I may learn at last to keep my own in every situation in life. To discover and create in myself, as I grow old, that thing which is to life what style is to letters, moral radiance."

The esthetic equivalent of that kind of salutary shock is reflected in the "violent annunciation" "from above" which, as Yeats says in his note to "Leda and the Swan," prompted his writing of that poem. The wisdom that the speaker in the poem ascribes to the swan, and which makes him question whether a similar understanding can be imparted to Leda and, through her, to her semi-divine progeny—this wisdom is actually grounded in the temporary abasement of the godhead, as well as in the surrender of girlish innocence and in the fall of a noble house and proud city. All of which have their equivalents in Yeats's Ireland. It may be the persistence of such barriers—delineating the separation between God, soul, and world—which keeps the self from becoming whole. All three might be married in an instant by the primal force of the imagination. And only what remains apart, whether in pride or innocence, would stand to be further reduced by the imagination. This is the knowledge that seems only imperfectly to have been imparted to Yeats's Leda.

We may reasonably expect that the pliant energy of the speaker in "Leda and the Swan" will become not only even more lyrically refined, with a poem like "High Talk," but also more poignantly deflated—with the "rag-and-bone" philosophy of "The Circus Animals' Desertion." The strength of Yeats's imagination seems thus to consist of the poet's continual attempt to resolve the differences separating the physical and the spiritual self; and "Leda and the Swan" is Yeats's monumental attempt to give mythic dimension to the problem through a profound psychological artistry.

Images tangle with each other beneath the formal patterning of "Leda and the Swan," rising, as it were, to the archetypal occasion in their expression of violence. By this means the speaker is trying, psychopoetically, not simply to recreate, but to explode the myth as an external event. In analyzing the "real" occasion for the poem," we may conclude that the contending images which constitute the mythic scene are the imaginative redressing of an earlier "dissociation of sensibility." The imagery of violence projected in verbal form does not point to historic or mundane phenomena, the disparate world of things and events, so much as it suggests dissolving "borders" of "a single mind, a single energy" which the poet believes "can be evoked by symbols."

chapter 7

contemplation and excitement:
the overriding vision in six late poems

We may consider finally six of Yeats's late poems—"Among School Children," "Byzantium," "Lapis Lazuli," "The Statues," "High Talk," and "The Circus Animals' Desertion"—in which the speaker attempts to resolve by some climactic image or gesture the close opposition between Daimon, self, and world. The speaker emerges as the principal figure in this trichotomy, testing against the flux of time and place his insights into the permanence of *Anima Mundi*. The person of the speaker is what is most subject to radical change, and the achievement in each of these poems is measured by the personal transformation the speaker effects with his ordering of images in the poem. In its most inspired moments the poetry rises above the level of contemplation, but in each case the contemplated image or imaginative setting lays the ground for the impact of the speaker's final vision.

What we want to concentrate on then in each of these six lyrics is the invisible matter of the poetic imagination. The facet of Yeats's poetry that is most remarkable is that which shows the image dissolving into the gathering volume of words: as this happens the more sensitive we become to the dominating force of the speaking voice. And we should not be surprised if, in the end, in "The Circus Animals' Desertion," the poem leaves us aware of the quite solitary presence of the speaker.

We may proceed with our inquiry asking by what means the memorable image or gesture terminating the poems satisfies the preparatory tension—spiritual or esthetic—built into the body of the poem.

In "Among School Children" the speaker addresses himself to the world of imagination as an alternative to the delimiting existence of the world—people, things, ideas—confronting him in the classroom of a parochial school.¹ As he contemplates the scene in front of him he becomes transported beyond the classroom into a sphere entirely dictated by poetic vision.

Let us trace the progression. As he watches the pupils, taught to "be neat in everything," the speaker is reminded of days past when he and his beloved were children. Because she had exemplary beauty he can feel her presence among the girls now before him. "Even daughters of the swan [e.g., Helen] can share / Something of every paddler's heritage."

Though he and the beloved are old now, she "hollow of cheek" and he a "kind of old scarecrow," he muses how they both were joined in "youthful sympathy," and how he complemented her Ledaean beauty later on by cutting a figure of his own: "I . . . / Had pretty plumage once. . . ." And thought of this makes him, half-wistful, return a smile to those around him.

The "old nun" with her ward of children reminds him of his own "youthful mother"; and the children staring up at a "sixty-year-old smiling public man" set him musing as to what his mother might think could she but see her child now, sixty winters on his head. Does one reap the wind, after all?

The speaker sympathetically assumes the point of view of mother, child, teacher. Can the pang of giving birth, the painful maturing, the discipline one hands down, be nothing but fruitless labor? The icon the nun worships, the memories and expectations of a mother, the representation by artist or lover of some incomparable beauty—whatever images command one's faith—these, the lover implies, will only haunt their devotees with something the world here and now cannot satisfy. In this sense they are "self-born mockers of man's enterprise." ² If such things are to have value they must somehow take possession of the material scene, not constitute a separate reality—born out of pure beauty or blind devotion.

In the famous and ambiguous last stanza of the poem the speaker manages to remove himself from the setting which occasions his meditation. He leaves off the multiple point of view: talking about the uncertainties of youth and age, juxtaposing past and present, concrete reality and imaginative reminiscence. Instead he looks to a visionary unity.

In the first half of the last stanza he recasts what he has been reflecting upon in the form of a Self-sustaining wisdom. He intimates epigrammatically what is left out of the discipline or love not founded upon a holistic "passion, piety, or affection" (l. 54):

> Labour is blossoming or dancing where
> The body is not bruised to pleasure soul,
> Nor beauty born out of its own despair,
> Nor blear-eyed wisdom out of midnight oil.

Let one concentrate on books, place all hope in salvation, or demean the body—and one is put at the mercy of his means, cut loose of all but belief in some extrinsic reality. Unless a man can prove the mystery of his own being, his spiritual labors will only incapacitate him for life.

Spiritual power is for Yeats the power of the imagination to transform the self. It is the incarnate soul, like Valéry's dancer: awakened from its earthly element and capable of living "completely at ease, in an element comparable to fire—in a most subtle essence of music and movement." Such realization of imaginative power is, like the dance (according to Valéry), "that exaltation and that vibration of life . . . making what is divine . . . shine before our eyes." [3]

The image of the dancer in "Among School Children" represents the perfection of physical and spiritual grace, "unity of being," as Yeats puts it. While the correlative image of the tree signifies a stationary, undifferentiated power and beauty, the dancer suggests a "rhythmic body"; her movements reveal a living beauty that is entirely unselfconscious. The poem in the final lines symbolically shapes itself into a question, picturing the spiritualized form—tree or body—as an intensity no ordinary knowledge can comprehend.

> O chestnut-tree, great-rooted blossomer,
> Are you the leaf, the blossom or the bole?
> O body swayed to music, O brightening glance,
> How can we know the dancer from the dance?

And here once more (see "Demon and Beast") we have an instance of the contemplated reality converted into imaginative excitement. The seven previous stanzas shift between the visual scene and the visionary reality; with the last stanza the speaker's attention seems wholly absorbed by the envisioned unity of tree and dancer.

But how durable is the culminating image of the dancer? In analyzing "The Double Vision of Michael Robartes" Frank Kermode claims that the dancer "reconciles antithetical movements: the division of soul and body, form and matter" [4] and, we may add, in "Among School Children," the division between being and knowing. As Kermode points out, the dancer belongs to "Phase 15" of *A Vision*. It is the midpoint in the evolution of the self, and represents a perfection of movement, body, form—a "musical" and "sensuous" resiliency in which "will and thought, effort and attainment" are felt to converge (*V,* 135). The dancer as symbol implies a perfection of entrancing beauty, a sensible form wholly antithetical to the limitless and supersensual plasticity of "Phase 1."

It is "Phase 1," however, that constitutes "the final link between the living and more powerful beings" (*V,* 183), and which puts the self in immediate touch with both *Anima Mundi* and the self's spiritual Daimon. The images of tree and dancer are complete in their own right, the natural form or the esthetic element totally circumscribed by their perfection. Around their presence, therefore, the world would seem to turn. Yet they have not the daimonic power to become invisible to the world—in the unifying embrace of their transpersonal being. Tree and dancer are the paragons of those sensuous images which Yeats claimed must be dissolved if the body is ever to be set free of its self-evolving energy.

"Phase 1," no less than "Phase 15," can never be totally realized. They are states of imagined perfection, and the most the speaker can do is expend his energy in the expression of one rather than the other of these ideals. That, it seems to me, is the point of the speaker's enigmatic questioning at the end of "Among School Children."

The self relinquishes belief in an external reality by evolving toward an ultimate, innate wisdom. On the one hand, the speaker in "Among School Children" apostrophizes the images of "body," "tree," and "dancer" as an expression of the unity that takes charge of the poetic setting. In this respect no anxiety or sense of separation is implied in the question "How can we know the dancer from the dance?" But on the other hand, the speaker is concerned with finding out what the self-delighting image cannot reveal. And this is what arouses consternation. He wants to "know" the dancer as he might want to know himself; and reading the passage this way the speaker would seem to us to be trying to outgrow his sensuous involvement with image or form. The double apostrophe—"O body swayed to music, O brightening glance"—is therefore possibly reflexive; it may be construed to direct attention not to the sensuous beauty merely, "body" or "music," or even to an ostensibly physical movement, but to a quickening of insight. If we allow that the speaker no less than the dancer is moved by a "brightening glance" (the word "glance" has physical as well as ocular reference), then we see that the sensuous image is finely countered, if not subsumed, by a perceptual image of striking intensity.

We may do well to concede that "Among School Children" is, as Cleanth Brooks suggests, "finally a poem 'about' the nature of human imagination."[5] The poem appears to resolve the influx of images upon the creative imagination, forming for the person of the speaker a moment of illumination.

Paradoxically, the speaker's illumination takes the form of a disquieting stillness. "Images have but a borrowed life," Yeats maintains in "Anima Mundi" (*M,* 357). Along with ideas, as he goes on to say, images reflect continual opposition, though they may be urged always toward a "condition of fire" where all is "music and . . . rest." "The ultimate reality must be all movement, all thought, all perception extinguished" (*Ex,* 307). For Yeats the self is cleansed in the process of creation; the speaker concentrates intently on the inimitable image which heralds his personal transformation. Not the image, however, but the imaginative force projecting the image gives direction to this transforming process. "We . . . are certain," he says, in his diary of 1930, "that nothing can give dignity to human nature but the character and energy of its expression. We do not even ask that it shall have dignity so long as it can burn away all that is not itself" (*Ex,* 339-40). In these terms the aim of the poet in "Among School Children" may be best understood: the poem seems to want to focus finally on the ecstasy and the uncertainty of the speaker rather than on images—however brilliant— which serve to precipitate his conflicting emotion. Those apostrophized images of dancer and tree stand too blissfully apart from the immediate setting of the poem to offer the speaker anything more than a questioning reflection of his unfulfilled relationship to a chosen ideal.[6]

Something of this same dilemma and ambiguity may be found in "Byzantium," the celebrated poem Yeats wrote in 1930, four and a half years after "Among School Children." It, too, centers attention on the life of the imagination, and it may be as C. S. Fraser suggests: the poet achieves immortality in the poem as a work of art.[7] It would be a mistake however to think that Byzantium is for Yeats an abiding symbol. It is a means rather than an end of artistic creation. And its place in the schematic framework of *A Vision* marks only one of a number of possible representations of an unreachable perfection.

The succession of images which compose "Byzantium" are meant to distill, not stratify, the subject of the poem. The final lines impress upon the poem the curious irony of its subject—the artist's arraignment of the imagination. The poet seems to be concerned in the end with the viability of the speaker's spiritual impulse. As early as 1909, thinking perhaps of Blake's Jerusalem and then of the miscarriage of the metaphysical reality in *Oisin,* Yeats insisted that "we must renounce the deliberate creation of a kind of Holy City in the imagination, and express the individual" (*A,* 335). In 1910 Yeats's visit to Mont St. Michel made him wonder if that isolated town did not house the "marvellous powerful living" art created by the ideal culture.[8] By 1910 he had quite given up the idea that contemporary Dublin could embody the unity of culture he had envisioned for that city. In 1923, when he received the Nobel Prize, he dwelt on the possibility of Stockholm being the chosen city. And we have the first mention of the marvels of Byzantium when he compares the latter to Stockholm (*A,* 374).

In 1930 Yeats could certainly maintain that the subject for the poem "Byzantium" had "been in my head for some time" (*Ex,* 290). But since his system and his overall view argue against any fixed symbol, Byzantium, like any other ideal city, can only provisionally be construed as a "Holy City of the imagination." It is indeed the "individual," as Yeats said, the self in the process of change, that should command principal attention in his poetry. And perhaps the images in the poem "Byzantium" are best interpreted if seen in a molting relationship to the self.

In commenting on the mythopoetic significance of Byzantium, Yeats reveals the humanistic implications of his esthetic principles. Practitioners of the ancient art of Byzantium, he wrote in an oft-quoted passage in "Dove or Swan," tend through art to remove the material object from the sphere of physical influence. Artists serve as an example to those who would manipulate for power in the physical world, and lay claim to earthly demesnes in their messianic search for the absolute. For Yeats the individual who comes closest to a realization of spiritual power is the unassuming, virtually anonymous "philosophical worker in mosaics." He transforms in the company of others like him all personal ambition, lavishing on the raw material of art the refinement and discipline that grows from an unassertive mode of expression.

The transparency of the worker's hand is evident in what he does because he has "the supernatural descend" to him in his double effort to transcend form and remake himself. With consummate application "the pride of his delicate skill would make what was an instrument of power to princes and clerics . . . show as a lovely flexible presence like that of a perfect human body" (*V*, 279). The ideal artist can be distinguished from his art no more than can the dancer be distinguished from her dance.

The artist of Byzantium has allowed himself to become the instrument of an unconscious power, containing but not restricting his means of expression. His ability is demonstrated by an artful grace and ease. For this reason Yeats would consign him and his kind to "Phase 15," the same visionary category as that of the dancer (*V*, 281).

But in *A Vision* Yeats is careful to point out that the "worker in mosaics" is a philosopher no less than an artist, and as a result can remain content only so long with that "musical" and "sensuous" perfection of the human body associated with "Phase 15." The "philosophical worker" is a "somnambulist" of the imagination, as Yeats says, whose "profound reverie" discloses an intangible presence, a motionless awareness of his "sensuous dream" (*V*, 281, 283). He is just on the verge of that supernatural awareness ("Phase 1") by which he may finally be free of the mind's endless proliferation of image. Similarly, in consort with his peers, the artist works to make of the images peculiar to his culture a "single image": an immaterial unity which fulfills his own sense of being by enabling him to understand thoroughly the limitations of the human condition. This is the state "in which men have attained the supreme miracle and loved one another" (*A*, 375).

It is quite possible to regard Yeat's somnambulist as the speaker in "Byzantium" and the somnambulist's vision as reaching toward realization of the "complete passivity, complete plasticity" of "Phase 1." [9] There is general agreement among critics in following the lead of Cleanth Brooks [10] and assigning to the speaker a position between the two unreachable apogees of the self, "Phase 15" and "Phase 1." These are designated in the poem by "a starlit [moonless] or . . . moonlit dome"; the dome ambiguously describes the palace roof, or the dome of Santa Sophia, or else the heaven overseeing the speaker's night in Byzantium. [11]

Yeats himself is quite explicit describing the "double mind" of the somnambulist. It is a mind "created at full moon" and the full moon "that now concerns us is not only Phase 15 of its greater era but the final Phase 28 of its millennium" (to be climaxed by return to "Phase 1"). Yeats also offers a picture of the double nature of Byzantium: "If I were left to myself I would make Phase 15 coincide with Justinian's reign, that great age of building in which one may conclude Byzantine art was perfected; but the meaning of the diagram [*V,* 266] may be that a building like St. Sophia, where all, to judge by the contemporary description, pictured ecstasy, must . . . precede the moment of climax" (*V,* 281–82). In the ecstasy induced by art the spiritual Daimon urges human consciousness toward the "moment of climax." The ecstasy is an unravelling of the conscious self, a trance state impelled by but attempting to work free of any thought or image-making sequence.

As Yeats describes it in "Phase 15" of *A Vision,* the trance is an "immovable" state: the body seems transfixed by the mind's eye. Depending upon his depth of concentration the communicant may get rid of hate and desire, putting off those thoughts which feed upon the world to prove the self's identity. All such thoughts are resolved into images which have "bodily form," and these in turn give way to the objects and beings from which they have been derived, so that the latter for the first time are regarded in their own right, unmindful of any assertion of the self.

Such objectivity is effected by the worker-in-mosaic's labor of love, and his example seems to have inspired the somnambulist's vision in "Byzantium": the somnambulist stands by as an immovable witness to his and man's spiritual estate. The succession of images in "Byzantium" breaks from an initial pattern of opposition between the natural and the supernatural to converge upon the source, the still-center of their poetic and psychological expression. The speaker's expenditure of energy within the poem for this reason lends itself to the expression of a progressive release of image and self.

The pattern of movement in the poem effectively culminates with projection of the illusory image of the "dancing floor." The tesselated "marbles" of which the floor is made at once compose and break up the images we are meant to see.

In imposing the verbal over the pictoral pattern the speaker would seem to dispel the purely visual image, substituting for it a sensuous awareness of its spiritual counterpart; in this way the natural becomes one with the supernatural, a marriage miraculously consummated by the artist:

> Astraddle on the dolphin's mire and blood,
> Spirit after spirit! The smithies break the flood. . . .

The smithies who "break the flood" work either in gold or in gold mosaic. To "break the flood" is an image that puts within reach as a correlative for artistic energy (the "flow" of imagination) the image of a seemingly less manageable medium, "that gong-tormented sea." The "flood" may therefore be construed as the gold poured into its mold or as the fluid contained in marble. And so "break the flood" may mean not only "to stop" but "to induce" to flow.[12] The masterpiece of the worker who constructs images of gold is the miraculous bird planted on a golden bough; and the product of the mosaic worker is a variable aquatic pattern in the "dancing floor." These parallel images of artistic form are thus made to reflect upon their origin, in nature as in the imagination, suggesting fixity and movement as an interchangeable process in the realm of art.

It is apparent that these achievements of the artificer are dissimilar if not opposite in kind.

The golden bird, whose image is developed in stanza 3, has a shifting temperament. Meant to represent alternately "Phase 1" and "Phase 15," he appears petulantly out of phase. He crows and scorns common birds as though, in spite of himself, his idealized nature fell short of absolute control. Seen in this light, the golden bird is an ironic symbol of perfection. The symbol shows an obvious discrepancy between the ultimate reality and the manner or form in which it is represented, pointing, as Richard Ellmann says, to "the two directions of [Yeats's] own art."[13] And that discrepancy between the fixed and organic image also accounts for the related symbol in stanza one, the "starlit or moonlit dome," whose composure is too perfect to keep it, or else the speaker, from "disdaining / All that man is."[14]

In stanzas 2, 4, and 5 the disgruntled attitude gives way because the absolute is not conceived apart from the living form. It is the image rather than the symbol which the speaker concentrates on in those stanzas. The image does not solidify into symbol and as a result is more resilient.

Contrasted to the fixed aloofness of "dome" and "bird" in stanzas 1 and 3 we have in stanzas 2 and 4 an evolutionary repetitiveness of image.[15] The syntax in these alternate stanzas, conspiring with the rhyme, rhythm, and alliteration of the verse line, suggests the intended mystery by a virtually hypnotic circularity of language. Verbal movement of this kind is hardly amenable to the stationary symbols, "bird" and "dome." In stanzas 2 and 4 the repetition ends in a paradoxical inversion of sense and image—

[13] A mouth that has no moisture and no breath
[14] Breathless mouths may summon;
[15] I hail the superhuman;
[16] I call it death-in-life and life-in-death.

[25] At midnight on the Emperor's pavement flit
[26] Flames that no faggot feeds . . . .
[27] . . . . flames begotten of flame,
[28] Where blood-begotten spirits come
[29] And all complexities of fury leave,
[30] Dying into a dance,
[31] An agony of trance,
[32] An agony of flame that cannot singe a sleeve.

We are mindful of the verbal inversion of line 16; the paradoxical tautology of lines 26–27; the invertible syntax of lines 13–14; the optional syntax of line 31 ("agony" as an appositive of "dance" in line 30 or as the direct object of "leave" in line 29)—all contributing to a metaphysical elusiveness of statement. In the process the visual image seems converted to its spiritual referent.

In the fifth and final stanza the image is given new life. The repetition there suggests a more strenuous accommodation of the natural to the supernatural environment, with the result that the original setting of the poem undergoes a kaleidoscopic change. The alternate composing and fragmentation of image suggested by the image of the dancing floor reflects what Yeats called "marmorean stillness," the still movement or dynamic stasis of the somnambulist's dream. Images succeed, in the process of counteracting, each other, so that there is finally a genuine confusion between the pictorial and the psychological scene:

Marbles of the dancing floor
Break bitter furies of complexity,
Those images that yet
Fresh images beget,
That dolphin-torn, that gong-tormented sea.

The poem closes with a bristling ambiguity. "Those images" are to be construed in opposition to both "marbles of the dancing floor" and "bitter furies of complexity," the subject and the direct object respectively of the word "break." The sentence reads to suggest continual renewal and dissolution of two types of image, the image transformed into art and the image which is disconcertingly subjective. The terminal image, "that dolphin-torn, that gong-tormented sea," consequently shifts our focus from the representational form (mosaic? golden statuary? of the dolphins) to the psychological torment of the speaker himself. The ecstasy which begets art is able merely to counter the speaker's agonizing self-awareness. For this reason the process to which the poem testifies can do no more than adduce evidence of a perpetual struggle for release.

The repetitive pattern of stanza 5 does not aim to cap the poem with a change-resistant image. It serves only to return the reader back through the poem, to reconsider the terms of separation set up in stanzas 1 and 3: between images depicting the luminous miracle of "bird" or "dome" and those images, depicting "complexities of mire and blood," in which originates man's spiritual dilemma. Scornful separation of the physical and the spiritual is ironically represented by the static beauty of miraculous symbols. But "Byzantium" is primarily an image-making, image-breaking, not symbol-based, poem. The poem does not express something that pretends to the impossible, but develops organically. Byzantium, with its palace, cathedral, golden bird, and celestial dome, is a prestructured symbol which readily catches the imagination, but which leaves the speaker to design out of his sequence of restive and paradoxically fleeting images a more humanly compelling structure.

As a poem "Byzantium" demonstrates that the imagination is both a constructive and a destructive force. The poem is the illusory form the passing images take, the dream, as it were, of a perfection that cannot be realized. It is not any visible form or external unity (in or beyond time and place) that "Byzantium" expresses. Rather, the poem registers the antipodal relationship between images as that relationship bears on the state of mind of the speaker. The referents of images are swallowed up as the intensity of the mind ordering those images concentrates upon its own evolution. In this respect "Byzantium" moves toward the same kind of ending as does "Among School Children," "Leda and the Swan," and "The Second Coming." In each of these late poems the question of spiritual evolution is felt to hinge ultimately not upon any fixed image but upon the sheer force of the speaker's imagination. The same is true of other poems written after "Byzantium" whose manner of expression might otherwise be thought evidence of their author's predilection for violence.

For Yeats (as for Blake and Shelley) self-destruction is proportionate to realization of the superhuman awareness of Self. It depends upon the simultaneous exhaustion of moral considerations and personal desire, ultimately leaving the poet and life without any claim upon each other. Having behind him his particular flare of success in the world, Yeats, by the last decade of his life, could well afford to take stock of the ironic role of poets and poetry. With his gusto increasing the older he became, Yeats visualized the collapse of physical reality as a way to strengthening the spiritual imagination. And the poem as the most pointed medium of the imagination seemed to press for some form of liberation. We may consider this matter in treating a sequence of three poems. They illustrate Yeats's long-deliberated notion of "tragic joy" and prepare for the brilliantly antithetical moods of "High Talk" and "The Circus Animals' Desertion."

Yeats first talked of "tragic joy" in relation to the theater, conceiving of drama, no less than the act of the mind, as a counterpoise to action in the physical world. (See, for example, "Lapis Lazuli.") [16] In 1911, in *Plays for an Irish Theatre,* Yeats noted that the watchful reverie of the somnambulist's dream—a possible state of mind for poet, dramatist, or actor—becomes the condition of "tragic pleasure." [17] A year earlier, in the essay "J. M. Synge and the Ireland of his Time," Yeats spoke of "the artist's joy" as being potentially "of one substance with that of sanctity," its virtue consisting in "the delight of expression" as the actor or poet displays the spoils of spiritual "warfare" (*E, 321*).

What the artist evolves from "warfare" in the visible and the invisible world (the mind) makes indeed for a "noble art." And "the sacrifice of a man to himself" culminates for the artist the advantages won in battle (*E, 321*). The struggle in the last analysis is an internal one. Conor Cruise O'Brien, having examined Yeats's seeming proclivity to Fascism in the twenties and thirties, came to a similar conclusion: that the ideology of politics and the ways of the world, however related to, clearly are not the belief and the way of, the visionary poet.[18] As pointed out earlier, the play *The Unicorn from the Stars* (1902, 1908) shows Yeats writing about the physical or historical reality in relation to the invisible world, focusing attention on the mind as it deals with its self-appointed problem: identifying the very state of "consciousness with conflict" (*V, 214*).

Yeats's concern with the action of the mind has special relevance in "Meru" and in the two other late poems, "The Gyres" and "Lapis La-

zuli," which follow in sequence in *The Collected Poems.* Published in
1934, "Meru" is the last of the *Supernatural Songs* addressed to the ro-
bust spirit of the hermit-saint. In the poem the speaker is concerned
with the sanctity the mind achieves isolated from the "manifold illusion" of civilized life, and provides us with some basis for comparing the
saint's virtue with the métier of the artist. "The poet writes always of
his personal life," Yeats said in 1937, "in his finest work out of its tragedy" (*E,* 509). The poet may be the triumphantly articulate victim of
his own designs on life. Though he can never completely insulate himself from life, he takes to expressing his passion and finds the personal
involvement in his fate thereby diminished. He would agree with the
speaker in "Meru" in maintaining that life can never be free of conflict,
and that, so long as material effects abound, peace among men is simply
an illusion. Insofar as "man's life is thought" one can try overcoming his
purely sensuous nature by "Ravening through century after century /
Ravening, raging, and uprooting that he may come / Into the desola-
tion of reality" (*P,* 563). The moment of truth is wrought by the self-
eradicating action of the mind, and that moment is what lays bare to the
eye the proliferating illusion of the world. Civilization, the speaker implies, is the materializing effect of man's thought, and as such multiplies
and memorializes his ambitions, desires, and moral involvement. The
energetic indifference of the saint to man's fate is what brings his soul to
the saving heights of "Mount Meru or Everest."

But how tenable is that kind of ascent? The poet, unlike the saint, is
not bent on his own salvation. He is more concerned with perfecting his
art as a way of life. Because the self-relinquishing discipline of art brings
into perspective the human condition, the poet would even be willing to
"live it all again" (*P,* 479). The personal tragedy is conceived as an occasion for joy, and this may be communicated through art if not through
life itself. The rejoicing tragedian thus takes the saint one step farther
and shows the millennium he is after to be a continuation of, rather than a
separation from, life. The "dawn" the speaker in "Meru" looks forward
to may in fact be that entirely inward state which enables one to survive
without escaping the endless ravaging of time.

"The Gyres" and "Lapis Lazuli," the first two poems in Yeats's last
volume of verse,[19] articulate the artist's rather than the saint's tragic encounter with life. In "The Gyres" the speaker in his excitement is not
caught up or deterred by any one tragic image. He expresses a passionate detachment from all the circumstances of heroic disaster that he

cares to catalog. He rides the crest of man's fall, and would seem to call into question even the aspirations of mind and imagination. Old ideas, and old forms, like old civilizations, cannot vie with their initial vigor. ". . . Look forth; / Things thought too long can be no longer thought, / For beauty dies of beauty, / Worth of worth, / And ancient lineaments are blotted out" (*P,* 564). If a man's attention is turned to nothing in particular, only then may he be fulfilled of his purpose and his responsibility in life. "If our works could / But vanish with our breath," the speaker says in "Nineteen Hundred and Nineteen," "that were a lucky death. / For triumph can but mar our solitude" (*P,* 431). The poem itself, as an occasion for celebration, brings with it its own paradox. "What's the meaning of all song?" asks the speaker in "Vacillation." " 'Let all things pass away,' " comes the ironic reply (*P,* 502).

But the end of all things is not annihilation. It is a recreation of the spirit in terms of what this world must ever leave unfinished. "Those that Rocky Face [the anti-self? [20]] holds dear / . . . shall . . . / From . . . rich, dark nothing disinter / The workman, noble and saint" (*P,* 564–5) It is not the heights but the depths of reality that remain to be scaled. The imposts of time have yet to drop from the eyes of the elect, to renew, by rerooting their lives on a terrestrial plane, the highest and the lowest of men together. The spirit of the world, *Anima Mundi,* continues to evolve as the mind fashions what men call reality, until "all things run / On that unfashionable gyre again"; the gyre returns civilization to the basic reality and the inexpressible mystery of life finds out its new (yet archetypal) exponents. Given that interminable cycle all Old Rocky Face "knows is that one word 'Rejoice!' " And "we that look on" mere ruin "but laugh in tragic joy." The self may thus escape from that slavish wheel of time, intellect, and moral constraint. Tragic joy is an expression of inner life transformed through time.

Of all Yeats's poems "Lapis Lazuli" gives us the most memorable image of tragic joy. The poem was written during the gathering storm of the second world war. The speaker scorns the danger that might be launched by "Aeroplane and Zeppelin"; for all he cares the town may "lie beaten flat." "Hysterical women" can scream all they want at "poets that are always gay." Whatever disaster occurs the poet knows has happened before.

In stanza 2 of the poem the scene shifts to the inner world of the stage. Every part may be so mastered that no tragedy, on the boards or real, may unnerve the actor. "Hamlet and Lear are gay," their tragedy subsumed by art. The throes or fears of those who play their parts are deftly put off. "Gaiety transfigur[es] . . . dread." The joyous tragedian is entirely rid of presumption, summoning only the energy with which he can readily fulfill his appointed role. No other ideal matters. By such means mask and being, drama and life, become one. The crucial scene, played to the hilt, provides its own sanctum: "Heaven blazing into the head: / Tragedy wrought to its uttermost."

The real battle, we learn, is the one fought for self-illumination. Poet, playwright, and tragedian are one in their attempt to liberate themselves from what is merely personal. In dramatizing they hope to transform *Hysterica Passio,* the mounting outrage that drives proud kings mad. They find that personal distance makes for dramatic immediacy. And this is what the consummate artist learns to communicate.

In the fall of a civilization visible evidence of the artist's work may well be wanting. But that possibly is the very thing which impels him to create. What survives is immaterial. For him life is not any artifact of reality but a source for spiritual renewal. "All things fall and are built again, / And those that build them again are gay."

The speaker controverts this principle, however, in the last stanza, with his meditation on a piece of precious stone. The picture of the three Chinamen, with their serving man, settling down on a hand-carved mountain is the serene but problematic climax of "Lapis Lazuli." The Chinamen are to be imagined there, staring "on all the tragic scene," their blithe spirits refusing any mournful epitaph. The "accomplished fingers" of the serving man play long-unheard melodies. And as a result the sages' eyes, "mid many wrinkles, / Their ancient, glittering eyes, are gay." With that vision the poem ends. The oriental pastorale fixed in stone turns out to be the poem's most memorable image, an example of the enlightening transposition effected through art.

But is this celebrated picture of "Lapis Lazuli" the most felicitous ending? The speaker appears to have been captured by the glittering image of that quiescent landscape, changing from the prime mover to the observer of the scene he creates. Yeats indeed had in his possession the lapis lazuli he writes about. Like Sato's sword he received it as a gift from an admirer of his. He sees in the precious stone carving the symbol of an esthetic wisdom and uses that symbol to cap his poem of tragic joy. In so doing, however, he signs off the vigor of the three previous stanzas.

The energy building up through "Lapis Lazuli" by the last stanza comes to a brilliant pass; but if our attention is held, our aroused feelings are not really satisfied, by the concluding symbol. That symbol does not grow out of the buoyant movement of images which precede. It is more an artifact of the imagination, made to survive the poem's spiritual progression. Rather than cross the stage himself, as it were, with some instinctive gesture, our speaker, it seems, has retired to his study, to present to us in his place the lucent composure of the three Chinamen.[21]

Two of the last poems Yeats wrote contrast with "Lapis Lazuli": "The Statues" and "High Talk." Both poems depend for their effectiveness upon the energy of the speaking voice, rather than upon a premeditated symbol. And both poems, like "Byzantium," work to dissolve the image under pressure of an unrevealed, Self-begotten mystery.

The sequence of images in "The Statues" is meant to suggest no fixed, visible, form, but the act of the imagination as it shapes its "proper dark." The work "in marble or in bronze" suffers from the disenchantment of an impassioned observer. A lover's lips cannot give life to "a plummet-measured face." And yet those reasoned calculations of the ancient worker in marble or bronze are made to subdue "all Asiatic vague immensities." The statues contain if not cancel in the semblance of "casual flesh" the incalculable mysteries of the East. The Apollonian tradition of classical art made into human form its mathematical ideal, the achievement of the mind bringing into order life's otherwise unmanageable multiplicity. What from the "many-headed foam" survived the battle between East and West was presumably put down by Phidias in his lovely dreams of women, forms of art delicately palpable to the imagination, virtually defying the substance they are made of.

Subsequently, the speaker tells us, "one image crossed the many-headed." The languishing idealism of the West was bound to give way to its counterpart in the East. The physical energy triumphantly expended at Salamis had gathered into itself the force it purported to defeat. Out of that fusion, between the one and the many, came the "fat / Dreamer of the Middle Ages," image of the spiritual plenitude of a world-encompassing mind.[22] In the Middle Ages, Yeats implies, reason started to unwind from its ethereal course and revert to the more tangible things of the spirit.

"When gong and conch declare the hour to bless / Grimalkin crawls to Buddha's emptiness." Lover and beloved, unsatisfied by any projected ideal, seek out their opposites, the image of something unknown. Nothing appears to them more terrible than the spiritual presence that destroys all illusion. Grimalkin may be the lunar cat Minnaloushe who "creeps through the grass," an abiding spirit who makes the "Lame Man blessed" (*PL*, 300, 302). Or Grimalkin may be girl or woman bewitched by dreams of love. However seen, her fate hinges upon "Buddha," a spiritual conjunction evinced by the fading consciousness of her own self.

"When Pearse summoned Cuchulain to his side, / What stalked through the Post Office? What intellect, / What calculation, number, measurement, replied?" The answer is: Nothing calculated can answer to man's communion with his fated image. No statue can do more than commemorate the terrifying moment of vision. The speaker numbers himself among that heroic, Celtic, elite of an age celebrated for its spiritual unity. For him that age spans the "spawning fury" of "this filthy modern tide."

Yet for all its formless multiplicity the contemporary world may still witness miracles. Those of us who "climb to our proper dark" may renew the example of Pearse, revitalize an inward strength. Heir to the enveloping spirit of the world, *Anima Mundi,* are those who build upon the past, all experience from Buddha to Pearse, from India to Ireland, bringing form to what is formless by the unique ordering of their spiritual understanding. And that too is what gives moment to the evolutionary intensity of the poet's imagination.

The speaking voice is what commands the most attention in Yeats's poetry. And it is the speaking voice which so fashions the image that we are made to incline our ear rather than train the eye to what is being said. If dynamic enough the voice can hold the world in breathless sway, the impelling force of the speaker's imagination bringing the listener beyond what is merely visible. No one image retards the imagination in actualizing this force; each image is served up, so to speak, to heighten the imagination. The total effect is to make what is "seen" appear transparent to the eye.

This is the point of view that has been brought to bear on Yeats's late poems. "Lapis Lazuli," we have argued, while symbolizing, falls short of actually demonstrating the transparency of image in the poem. The interchangeable image of the dancer and the dance in "Among School Children" more nearly demonstrates the perspicuous point of view in that poem, but the unforgettable image in the last stanza moves in its own medium without appearing to have evolved organically from the meditational complexities in the preceding stanzas. "Byzantium"

shows the process by which images replete with movement, and representing an agonizing imperfection, are played off against the scowling,
static images of perfection; it is a poem in which the laboring process of
creation rather than a lucid sense of fulfillment is depicted. The same is
true of "The Statues." There the poet strains to take account of He-
gelian opposites, and as a result the cerebral vies with the imaginative
representation of the liberating cycle which the poem, as process, describes. "The Statues" comes nearest, though, to dissolving the poem's
central image, substituting for the meditative symbol of "statues" the
uplifting genius of the speaker's spiritual solitude.[23] All four poems,
thus considered, point the way to our discussion of "High Talk," perhaps the most remarkable and most neglected of Yeats's lyrics.

"High Talk" is certainly the least self-conscious of Yeats's middle
and late poems, sporting words with a disarming show of simplicity. It
is par excellence a poem of exultation, affording its speaker at the end
perhaps the most delightfully extravagant gesture of any Yeats poem.
The tour de force of Yeats's last years, "High Talk" is also the happy result of five decades of esthetic-spiritual self-discipline. The speaker in the
poem is in complete control, able to energize the full range of his central
metaphor. The upshot of his argument might be paraphrased by this
line of Rilke's: "More than ever / The things we can live with are falling away, and their place / . . . taken by an imageless act."[24] The
words in Yeats's poem follow as a sheer veil upon the action the speaker
articulates.

B. L. Reid, the only critic who has made much of "High Talk," calls
the poem "astonishingly brilliant . . . unlike anything else in Yeats": a
kind of "absolute poem."[25] I follow Reid's lead in assuming the uniqueness of "High Talk," and wish to elaborate on his thesis by considering
the singular pitch of the images that Yeats uses in his poem.

"Processions that lack high stilts have nothing that catches the eye."
With that opening the speaker in the person of Malachi Stilt-Jack declares he will have high stilts and will make them do service they are
not ordinarily cut out for. The procession he leads follows an unearthly
course, overreaching the spirit of the mundane world. And his lineage
spotlights the world of the imagination. "What if my great grand-dad
had a pair [of stilts] that were twenty foot high," and "some rogue of
the world stole" [my] "fifteen foot" pair "to patch up a fence or a fire"?
His resources are such that they can outfit the imagination with what
only metaphorically holds the eye:

> Malachi Stilt-Jack am I, whatever I learned has run wild,
> From collar to collar, from stilt to stilt, from father to child.
> All metaphor, Malachi, stilts and all.

His blood traces an invisible line "from father to child," rejoicing in the
lead of those who came before him. He fulfills his own past by holding
an intrepid light to the future, all that life and the illustrious dead have
taught him catching fire from the imagination.

>   A barnacle goose
>   Far up in the stretches of night; night splits and the
>   dawn breaks loose;
>   I, through the terrible novelty of light, stalk on, stalk on. . . .

That fancied procession mentioned earlier, for women who "demand a
face at the pane" and for children who "demand Daddy-long-legs," is
only a prelude to his real calling. For all his talk Malachi never had
stilts to satisfy the crowd. They are his forebears, his would-be admirers,
and his progeny he is talking about, those as yet unsatisfied and unfulfilled because of their demands on life. For them he would "take to
chisel and plane," not to put himself on display but to fashion from
himself and all that he has learned such a train of words that would
capture the eye from any physical form, and from the interjection of
any self-centered reality:

>   I, through the terrible novelty of light stalk on, stalk on;
>   Those great sea-horses bare their teeth and laugh at the dawn.

The transfiguration of the speaker seems just in the offing with that resounding last line of the poem. The suggestion of any lesser reality is
overthrown by the image of "these great sea-horses," and their bright
laughter. In all Yeats's poetry nothing like this image comes so suddenly
upon the reader and yet appears so naturally as a climax to the poem. Its
emergence from what precedes is as uncanny as it is striking, lifted
above whatever temporal reference previous images might have had.

   In 1935 Yeats wrote to Ethel Mannin that "I want to plunge myself
into impersonal poetry, to get rid of the bitterness, irritation and hatred
my work in Ireland has brought into my soul. I want to make a last
song, sweet and exultant, a sort of Europe[a]n *geeta,* or rather my *geeta,*
not doctrine but song" (*L*, 836). Since 1935 Yeats had written "The
Gyres," "Lapis Lazuli," and "The Statues," poems quite free of "bitter-

ness, irritation and hatred," but these seem only a preparation for "High Talk."

That lyric, published just a month before Yeats's death, sings the kind of pure exultation the poet looked forward to in writing his *"geeta."* Just as earlier he wanted to get rid of all infinities and absolutes presupposing a reality other than that of the Self, so now he wanted to clear out of his writing anything that savored of personal response to the world around him. What he wanted his ultimate work to communicate was a freedom neither the individual personality nor the world could effect, a spiritual state loosed of all moral and material restriction; such a work would commend itself because of its unassuming force that disposes so brilliantly of its constituent elements. "The creation or enjoyment of a work of art," Yeats wrote in proposing a criterion for art, "is to escape from the constraint of our nature and from that of external things, entering upon a state where all fuel has become flame, where there is nothing but the state itself. Nothing to constrain or end it." [26] This is a fitting description of Yeats's accomplishment in "High Talk." That poem reaches its lyrical height relieved of all apparent constraint. Building upon as they move beyond any tributary image, the speaker's final words rise to an enduring gesture of release.

Yeat's temperament was not that of a mystic or platonic idealist. However high his spirit or imagination might propel him, he would be left to feel only more strongly the perishable substance of the material reality. In that consisted the real strength of his writing. He would let nothing except what he felt bodily determine the directing force of his imagination.

Yeats's work had its moments of lyric excitement. They occurred periodically, but could follow only upon a preparatory groundwork of observation and study. Poems of exultation naturally alternated with poems of wisdom and contemplation, as though continually to narrow the separation between body and mind, heart and soul, existence and being. Throughout we have evaluated Yeats's poems on the basis of their relative freedom from self-consciousness, calling attention particularly to the admixture in the speaking voice of spontaneous intensity and deliberative response. We have judged the persuasiveness of metaphor and image not in regard to the poet's aptitude for expressing the material object or external world but in terms of the poet's capacity to capture in poetry critical moments of self-possession.

Yeats himself constantly took account of his spiritual and poetic gains and put his case before the reader as frankly as imagination would allow. To many readers "The Circus Animals' Desertion" is the most astonishing of these self-evaluations in verse. In Yeats's final volume of verse the poem is placed quite decidedly after "High Talk" (the poem was published a month after "High Talk," and only a few weeks before Yeats died).[27] But the matter of chronology may well be incidental. Yeats's poetry moves through a succession of climaxes, the imagination giving birth to poems in its oscillation between always contracting points of opposition. And because Yeats was still "full of plans" when he died it would be a mistake for the reader to settle upon one poem as Yeats's final statement. The two poems in question for this reason are best considered as companion pieces rather than as incontrovertible cause and effect.

"The Circus Animals' Desertion," contrary in mood and conception to "High Talk," is a deliberative poem inspired by the speaker's unrelenting wisdom of defeat. The speaker sits commensal with the poet in reviewing his past. All sense of elation is gone. Fond memories suffer as the speaker-poet disengagingly tells of the supposed heights of his previous achievement. He harnesses his bandwagon of heroes and heroines to his own back and ironically draws the moral of their success. Oisin was "led by the nose" to undergo "vain gaiety, vain battle, vain repose" while he, the speaker-poet, "starved for the bosom of his faery bride." "My dear [who] must her own soul destroy," his modern prototype for the heroine of *The Countess Cathleen,* takes the place of his faery bride and proceeds, we are told, to make of "all my thought and love" an empty "dream." Cuchulain succeeds the figure of Countess Cathleen, treading the boards to rage against the sea, and proving in the end, like his faery bride and his immortal love, a no less slippery anodyne of the imagination.

No ideal preconception, no construct of the imagination can satisfy the poet's "love." The round of images he creates to enlarge his vision makes his mind out to be its own stumbling block. Everything he has done thus far to give substance to his imagination, he asserts without qualification, derives from the source of all illusion: "pure mind." And the recognition of that fact points to but one end.

> Now that my ladder's gone,
> I must lie down where all the ladders start,
> In the foul rag-and-bone shop of the heart.

In earlier poems the speaker had bemoaned "decrepit age" (*P*, 409) and had called on "singing-masters of my soul" to "consume my heart away" (*P*, 408). He would "compel . . . the soul to study / . . . / Till the wreck of body . . . / . . . / . . . come" (*P*, 416). But when the wheel turns full circle the body will not give in to the promise of any soulful abstraction. A new vigor develops from the combined energy of body and mind so that the imagination, as a result, bespeaks the inspiration of "an old man's frenzy" (*P*, 576). And final affirmation seems to depend on the thorough humbling of mind and body, the joint outposts of personal pride. Those "masterful images" that give reality to Niamh, Cathleen, and Cuchulain in the end have to give way. The iconoclast must break loose from the iconography shop of his own making, and overthrow every image that does not speak from "the heart."

The mind is made to honor, not spurn the body's decrepitude. A man rises to the occasion of his fate when, in struggling to walk free of the world, he acknowledges that there is no escaping the immediate demands of life. "The Circus Animals' Desertion" is not therefore a headhanging submission to defeat. By coming ever closer to grips with his mortality the speaker simply hopes to sweep the imagination clear of illusion.

"High Talk" and "The Circus Animals' Desertion" represent the logical conclusion to Yeats's commitment to an art of antithetical expression. The one poem is the climax to Yeats's poems of exultation, and the other the anticlimax to all his esthetic faith. Taken together the two poems demonstrate in their extremity the double function of the speaking voice: to serve as the composite agent and victim of its creator's poetic ideal.

Those poems beginning with "The Cap and Bells" and ending with "Leda and the Swan," "Byzantium," and "The Second Coming" culminate with a unique form of lyrical suspension in "High Talk"—neither confined to a world of dream, nor structured upon any disjunction between the visionary reality and the reality of life. For the first time the speaker's unflagging excitement absorbs into his vision images of the real world, bracing them to celebrate his self-liberating sense of delight. All the world about Malachi is caught up in the rush of his imagination and it is his transforming presence, not any fixed image, that makes for the crowning impact of the poem. Of the poems written after "The Cap and Bells" "High Talk" is the least self-conscious—the most fluent and most spontaneous—in expression.

But one is at a loss wondering how much farther in this direction the exultant speaker can take poetic language. "The Circus Animals' Desertion," with its seemingly existentialist base, provides the reader a more familiar measure of relief. In no previous poem of resignation or despair, from "The Cry of the Curlew" and "Adam's Curse" to the Crazy Jane poems and "Among School Children," does the speaker more relentlessly renounce all preconceptions. Ideas, images, high-minded ventures are regarded as so many expendable illusions, compared with the speaker's indelible self-awareness.

The voice of the poor forked creature in "The Circus Animals' Desertion" is too strong to summon up any image which will distract the speaker from the dreamer's fate. But because he has touched rock-bottom in expressing the reductive capacity of the self we need not suppose that therefore the dialectic of the speaker in the poetry as a whole would not have continued—collapsing all scaffolds which keep the spirit from outgrowing obstructing images: of the self, of the world, of some immaculate ideal.

"High Talk" and "The Circus Animals' Desertion" are both steps in the progress of the poet toward greater, not less, "responsibility"—to the potential (in spite of the absurdity) of the human condition. Even his final confrontation, with death, would seem to the poet proof not of the underlying emptiness of life but of the ultimate self-effacing strength of the imagination's spiritual fiber.

notes

1. C. M. Bowra seems to have had this view in mind when he contrasted Yeats to Valéry: "He [Yeats] is concerned not with the poet's ideal poem [*l'art pour l'art*] . . . but with his work and what it means to him"—*The Heritage of Symbolism* (London, 1962; originally published 1943), p. 29. F. A. C. Wilson regarded Yeats's concern with the Self as the distinguishing feature in his thought. "The main advance he [Yeats] made on other religious thinkers of the period lies clearly in his theory of the Self. . . . Religious thought at the turn of the century had attached itself to the concept of an externalized God. . . . Yeats almost alone perceived this truth ['the godhead within us'] for himself fifty years before the metaphysicians, and defended his isolated position with consummate integrity all his life"—*Yeats's Iconography* (London, 1960), pp. 20–21. Through their respective studies, *The Golden Nightingale: Essays on Some Principles of Poetry in the Lyrics of William Butler Yeats* (New York, 1949) and *The Identity of Yeats* (Oxford, 1954), Donald Stauffer and Richard Ellmann make reference to the "Self" as a psychological principle working through the poetry. The most consistent application of the principle of the Self as a criterion for judging the intensity of a poet's work is to be found in Priscilla Shaw, *Rilke, Valéry and Yeats: The Domain of the Self* (New Brunswick, 1964). For the latest treatment of "Self" in relation to symbolic expression, see Theodor von Klimek, *Symbol und Wirklichkeit bei W. B. Yeats* (Bonn, 1967), pp. 196 ff.

2. Yeats himself used the phrase "impersonal poetry" to refer to what I here call the "transpersonalizing voice"—that manner of expression which evolves from a feeling deeper than personal emotion: the ordering power of language or "song," as Yeats puts it, that is capable of "getting rid of the bitterness, irritation and hatred my work in Ireland has brought into my soul" (*L*, 836).

3. Yeats's attempt to live, think, and create from some fundamental belief in daimonic awareness is referred to by Ellmann as "affirmative capability." The term is used by Ellmann in contradistinction to Keats's term, "negative capability" (the capacity "of being in . . . doubts . . . without any irritable searching after fact & reason"), and in contrast to the spirit of modern writers who incorporate

skepticism into their poetry. For extended discussion of Yeats's daimonic sensibility, see Fahmy Fawzy Farag, "W. B. Yeats's Daimon," *Cairo Studies in English* (1961), 135–44. Farag claims that treatment of the two aspects of the Self in Yeats "did not originate, in the first place, from a division in Yeats's personality as Professor A. Jeffares insists" (p. 138). Yeats's daimonic awareness is conditioned by the desire to purge the Self of selfish emotions and to enlarge these to "vast passions." As Ernst Cassirer says, writing in 1923, in an intense state of "fear or hope, terror or wish fulfillment . . . the tension finds release, as the subjective excitement becomes more objectified, and confronts the mind as a god or a daemon"—*Language and Myth*, trans. Susanne Langer (New York, 1946), p. 33. But Yeats, contrary to Cassirer's implication here, is too sophisticated to believe the god or daemon is separate from the most intimate projection of human consciousness.

4. Yeats always identified the newspapers and journals with the "curiosities" of everyday life; they represented a concern for what is abstract and fragmentary rather than for what is "whole" and intrinsically valid.

5. "Music and Poetry," in *Broadsides* (Dublin, 1937), p. [x].

6. "Stillness" and "silence" are natural conclusions to any piece of writing, and as such may constitute an ironic comment on the function of artistic expression; but in "romantic" poetry the notions of "silence" and "stillness" may be incorporated into the language of the poem to suggest a metaphysical aftermath, and by this means seem to allow its form of expression to escape the impression of irony. See the "peak poems" of Wordsworth, "The Old Cumberland Beggar," "The Prelude, I ll.321 ff; XIV, ll.70 ff.; Coleridge, "Fears in Solitude," "Hymn Before Sunrise"; Shelley, "Hymn to Intellectual Beauty," "Mount Blanc"; Yeats, "The Cap and Bells," "Lapis Lazuli."

7. As Peter Ure says, the Noh "seemed to show how instinctively right [Yeats] had always been"—*Yeats* (Edinburgh, 1963), p. 89. Yasuko Stucki, however, feels that Yeats's concern with definite thoughts, in the plays he modeled after the Noh, contravene the very principle of Noh, which is to establish *Yugen,* the sense of emptiness common to aspirations of the yoga or Hinayana Buddhist, the divestment of all thought as a means for creating "the actual feeling of what a celestial world would be like in the mortal's imagination." The fault, Stucki maintains, is in the occult tradition of the West, which puts a premium upon the "Idea" as a vehicle for intuiting God—"Yeats's Drama and the Nō: A Comparative Study in Dramatic Theories," *Modern Drama,* IX (May 1966), 120, 122. Yeats of course had no intention of disregarding Gnostic tradition in the West; that tradition made him want to root his affirmation of spiritual reality in a necessarily more "concrete" psychological or even philosophical dramatic art.

8. *Language as Gesture: Essays in Poetry* (New York, 1952), p. 24.

9. The logical extension of this point of view for the reader and the critic is that set forth by Walter J. Ong in his argument for a fertile cross between the old personalist and the new critical approach to art or poetry: "each work of art is not only an object but a kind of surrogate of a person"—"The Jinnee in the Well-Wrought Urn," *Essays in Criticism,* IV (July 1954), 319.

10. "The Symbolic Imagination: The Mirrors of Dante," in *Collected Essays* (Denver, 1959), pp. 413, 419. My assumption that the artistic is related to the spiritual development of Yeats argues against such decidedly negative "early critics" of Yeats as D. S. Savage—"Inwardly he lacked the visionary intensity of the creative spirit, and his art developed peripherally, unaccompanied by any very interesting inward, personal development"—"The Aestheticism of W. B. Yeats," in *The Permanence of Yeats,* ed. James Hall and Martin Steinmann (New York, Collier Edition, 1961), p. 176—and Stephen Spender: "Yeats's poetry is devoid of any unifying moral subject, and it develops in a perpetual search for one"—"Yeats as a Realist," *Permanence of Yeats,* p. 169.

11. "Imagination is as the immortal God which should assume flesh for the redemption of mortal passion" (Shelley, Preface to *The Cenci*). "This world of Imagination is the world of Eternity; it is the divine bosom into which we shall all go after the death of the Vegetated body" (Blake, *A Vision of the Last Judgment*). The notion of the imagination as a redemptive form of incarnation derives from the Hellenistic gospel of St. John, and is central to Gnostic and romantic traditions. For a modern structuralist-humanist view of the poem as incarnation, see Murray Krieger, *A Window to Criticism: Shakespeare's Sonnets and Modern Poetics* (Princeton, 1964), pp. 33, 37, 68. For relation of the Gnostic and romantic traditions to mythic consciousness, see Northrop Frye, *The Anatomy of Criticism* (Princeton, 1957), especially pp. 122, 136.

12. See, for example, Yeats's statement, "There is no poem so great that a fine speaker cannot make it greater or that a bad ear cannot make it nothing" (*Ex, 212*). I find it difficult to accept MacDonald Emslie's argument that Yeats was "deceiving himself unconsciously" and that "[t]he voice in the poems is suspected of self-deceit"—"Gestures in Scorn of an Audience," in *W. B. Yeats, 1865-1965: Centenary Essays on the Art of W. B. Yeats* ed. D. E. S. Maxwell and S. B. Bushrui (Ibadan, 1965), pp. 103, 113.

chapter 2

1. Arthur Mizener was the first critic to make this point explicit ("The Romanticism of W. B. Yeats," in *Permanence of Yeats,* p. 125.

2. *What is Poetry* (New York, 1963), p. 33. Wheelock's proposal supplements T. S. Eliot's analysis in *The Three Voices of Poetry* (New York, 1954). Yeats's

concept constitutes a middleground between the Hindu and the Jungian concept of Self. Yeats did not share the Hindu aspiration to an absolute realization of Self apart from history or the ultimate condition of man; but unlike Jung he was not beyond speculating about the continuation beyond death of the individual human life (a notion familiar to the ancient Celts and revived for Yeats through his Rosicrucian studies and spiritualistic experiments). His preoccupation with the occult enabled him to imagine, like Blake, an infinite progress of the soul toward perfection. The perfection was an heuristic not an actual ideal of reality, allowing for a transpersonal, but not transcendental, endpoint in the history of the world and human affairs. For a similar view see Graham Hough, *The Last Romantics* (London, 1945), p. 260.

3. The speaking voice, as I use the term implies expression of a conscious or unconscious attempt to articulate the speaker's "anti-self"; the articulation gives form to the spiritual image that Ille, in "Ego Dominus Tuus," claims the objective artist is perpetually in search of. The term incorporates the more usual reference to tone and dramatic gesture—see Reuben A. Brower, *The Fields of Light: An Experiment in Critical Reading* (New York, 1951), p. 30—and offers a means of describing finally, as John Perry says, the "detailed and intimate experience the poem provides of a man being preeminently human"—"The Relationships of Disparate Voices in Poems," *Essays in Criticism*, XV (1965), 63.

4. Joseph Hone, *W. B. Yeats, 1865–1939* (New York, 1943), p. 41.

5. The ambiguity of emphasis is best explained by Horatio Krans, speaking of "The Lake Isle" among other poems: there is a "tendency that is in much of Mr. Yeats's verse, the tendency that is to slur the stress and to avoid emphatic rhythms. This is characteristic of Gaelic verse, and it is in the work of translators from the Gaelic—Mangan and others"—*William Butler Yeats and the Irish Literary Revival* (New York, 1904), p. 101. The slurring does not necessarily speed up the tempo in the verse, as the first of two recordings Yeats made of "The Lake Isle" for the BBC illustrates—*Poems*, Spoken Arts Recording #753 (New York, 1959). But neither is the tempo so relaxed that the poem, as James P. O'Donnell declares, need be earmarked for the fin de siècle, containing "an element of enervating weariness"—*Sailing to Byzantium: A Study in the Development of the Later Style and Symbolism in the Poetry of William Butler Yeats* (Cambridge, 1938), p. 131.

6. Sister M. Bernetta Quinn feels that the veils are "clouds," and that what is dropping from the clouds may be imagined to be a dove, a bird of peace—"Symbolic Landscape in Yeats: County Sligo," *Shenandoah*, XVI, 4 (1965), 44.

7. In his broadcast reading of the poem (1932) Yeats attempted to explain what he "must have meant" by the image "and noon a purple glow." He stated that it was the one ambiguous image in the poem: an image which revealed the peculiar feature of the island—"Innisfree" he translated "heather island," though

see Brandon Saul, *Prolegomena to the Study of Yeats's Poems* (Philadelphia, 1957), p. 54. The "purple glow," he supposed, was the reflection of heather in the water ("Poems," BBC Spoken Arts Recording #753).

8. "Notes to *The King of the Great Clock Tower*," in *The Variorum Edition of the Plays of W. B. Yeats*, ed. Russell K. Alspach and Catharine C. Alspach (New York, 1966), p. 109.

9. "Public Speech and Private Speech in Poetry," *Yale Review*, XXVII (March 1938), 544-45.

10. Conor Cruise O'Brien attempts to correct the prevalent assumption that it was because of Maud Gonne that Yeats became political-minded. Before he met Maud, Yeats was influenced by the high-minded nationalist politics of John O'Leary, but as O'Brien rather reluctantly points out, because of Maud, Yeats became more profoundly affected by the political scene in Ireland; and we may say that this deeper involvement of his as a result of his love for a woman would, of necessity, be reflected in his love poems. When Yeats decidedly backed off from the political scene in 1902, as O'Brien points out, his distance would result in a new kind of poetic comment—an aristocratic sangfroid—regarding the world around him—see Chapter 3 of this book; "Passion and Cunning: An Essay on the Politics of W. B. Yeats," in *In Excited Reverie*, ed. A. N. Jeffares and K. G. W. Cross (New York, 1965), pp. 212, 221-22

11. This evaluation agrees with that of Miss A. G. Stock, "The World of Maud Gonne," *Indian Journal of English Studies*, VI (1965), 59. Peter Ure takes the opposite stand, and contends that Yeats's own later impressions of the play— recorded in "The Irish Dramatic Movement" (*PC*, 89) and "The Circus Animals' Desertion"—belie its original intention (*Yeats*, p. 25). For illuminating discussion of the relation of Yeats's ideal prototype to historical circumstance and to Maud Gonne's historical role in playing the part of her prototype, see M. J. Sidnell, "Yeats's First Work for the Stage," in *Yeats, 1865-1965: Essays*, pp. 175 ff.

12. Virginia Moore, *The Unicorn* (New York, 1954), p. 425.

13. See *The Unicorn*, p. 179; Ellmann, *Identity of Yeats*, p. 76.

14. The poem is the first of several poems treated in this chapter which more or less illustrate David Daiches' proposition that "Nothing is more striking in Yeats's development as a poet than his gradual replacement of a two-term by a three-term dialectic." But in light of my explication of the early poems what Mr. Daiches goes on to say is highly questionable: that Yeats's "early poems are full of simple contrasts" and that only in the later poems is there any "resolution of opposites either in a *tertium quid* or else in a sense of the interpenetration of opposites." ("The Earlier Poems: Some Themes and Patterns," *In Excited Reverie*, p. 50). My feeling is that the speaking voice comes to be the *tertium*

quid even in the early poems, as it attempts to absorb the dichotomy of images or cope with the unresolved juxtaposition of opposites.

15. As S. B. Brushrui points out, the Daimon-demon are opposite sides of a single coin—originally conceived by the Greeks in a single word "Daimon," and gradually with the advent of Christ charged with the connotations of good and evil ("demon" is simply the Latin transliteration of the Greek). With its added meaning the Daimon-demon antinomy corresponds to the ambivalence of the faery in Celtic lore and of the Djinn in Arabic legend. For Yeats, it may be said, the Daimon (like the Djinn?) tends to preside over the poet's philosophic and artistic efforts as the elusive genius of his imagination ("Yeats's Arabic Interests," *In Excited Reverie,* p. 305). For an extended study see Farag, "Yeats's Daimon."

16. Thomas Parkinson, who offers the most extensive account of the revisions of the published versions of this poem, observes that in the 1925 version of the poem "Yeats presents not one point of view but three, ordered and organized for a single effect"—*W. B. Yeats, Self-Critic: A Study of His Early Verse* (Berkeley, 1951), p. 165.

17. *Ibid.,* p. 176.

18. *Ibid.,* p. 174.

19. F. A. C. Wilson discusses the significance of the tree imagery in Yeats's poetry (*Yeats's Iconography,* pp. 248 ff.).

chapter 3

1. Giorgio Melchiori reminds us that the pre-Raphaelite image of the rose gives way in the late nineties to the "typically decadent figure of Helen"—*The Whole Mystery of Art* (London, 1960), p. 118.

2. Professor Ellmann's contention (*Identity of Yeats,* p. 251) that this statement of Yeats is contradicted by the fact that the poem had to be revised, is not really valid. Yeats never enjoined spontaneity as the test of a poem's sincerity. By revising the poem Yeats must have thought he was bringing it closer to a fulfillment of its original intention.

3. As Vivian de Sola Pinto notes, "no intellectual meaning can be attached to [the] jester"—*Crisis in English Poetry, 1880-1940* (London, 1961), p. 95; and the same might be said of the queen.

4. What also contributes to the fluent movement of the verse line is the fluid syntax (evidenced by an abundance of articles, prepositions and conjunctions) and

high monosyllabic content (85 percent of the words in the poem are mono-syllabic).

5. Moore, *The Unicorn*, p. 202.

6. Jeffares, *Yeats, Man and Poet*, p. 60.

7. Although Conor Cruise O'Brien believes that Yeats's last prose work, *On the Boiler*, advocates "violent and suppressive practice" typical of fascism, he nonetheless concedes that as a young man Yeats was of "the school of John O'leary [which] withheld its endorsement from parliamentary action, frowned on agrarian agitation, and vehemently condemned acts of individual terrorism [the latter two being among the principles of Maud Gonne]—"Passion and Cunning," *In Excited Reverie*, pp. 213, 259. For an apology for Maud Gonne's espousal of violence ("There is no need to agree with her reasoning on physical force to recognize its lucidity"), see Stock, "The World of Maud Gonne," p. 66.

8. *Yeats, Man and Poet* (London, 1949), p. 67.

9. Maud Gonne MacBride, *A Servant of the Queen* (Dublin, 1938), p. 308.

10. *The Unicorn*, p. 202.

11. *Yeats, Man and Poet*, p. 101.

12. These and the following quotes, unless indicated otherwise, are from the sections of the "unpublished" autobiography printed in *Yeats, Man and Poet*, pp. 100–101, 266.

13. *The Unicorn*, pp. 37, 197 ff.

14. Quoted in *Yeats, Man and Poet*, p. 103.

15. *Ibid.*, p. 101.

16. Compare ll. 5–6 of the poem: "O what to me my mother's care, / The house where I was safe and warm . . ." with this statement of Yeats concerning his affair with Olivia: "I would be her first lover [i.e., extramaritally]. We decided that we should be friends till she could leave her home for mine but agreed to wait till her mother, a very old woman had died" (*Yeats, Man and Poet*, p. 101).

17. This listing agrees in part with Curtis Bradford's identification of the love poems with Maud Gonne and Olivia Shakespear, viz., "He tells of a Valley . . . ," "The Lover Mourns . . . ," and "He hears the Cry of the Sedge"—"Yeats and Maud Gonne," *Texas Studies in Language and Literature*, III (1961), 461 ff.

18. Yeats himself referred ironically to his notion of ideal love, in looking back to the influence of the Pre-Raphaelites. He wrote in his "unpublished" autobiography: "I would love one woman all my life. . . . I was a romantic, my head full of the mystical women of Rossetti, and those hesitating faces, in the art of Burne-Jones, which seemed always waiting for some Alcestis at the end of a long journey" (*Identity of Yeats,* p. 74).

19. Ellmann makes an interesting comment on this point: "In its careful contrivance, this poem holds back the person to whom it is addressed until the close, so that the sentence seems to struggle in the middle describing the travail, and to reach its difficult end simultaneously with the revelation of the object of such suffering" (*Identity of Yeats,* p. 67).

20. *Yeats, Man and Poet,* p. 118.

chapter 4

1. The corollary is, as George T. Wright states it, that "Yeats here presents himself, as never before, as an actual human being in an actual situation"—*The Poet in the Poem: The Personae of Eliot, Yeats, and Pound* (Berkeley, 1960), p. 105. Richard Ellmann quite pointedly shows the difference between the atmosphere of this poem and that of earlier poetry from *The Wind Among the Reeds,* by claiming "the possibility of reading it in either apocalyptic or climactic terms, and the impossibility of so reading the earlier ["The Secret Rose"], indicate Yeats's increasing mindfulness of his predominantly secular audience. . . . The poet emerges from his candle-lit room into the open air, and seems almost ready to stretch and rub his eyes in the light" (*The Identity of Yeats,* p. 103).

2. *Yeats, 1865–1939,* p. 164. Maud Gonne, in her autobiography, complained of her sister's too sensitive nature, and attributed it to her "passion for beauty." Kathleen "died, a faded white lily, after the son who came nearest to her ideal of beauty . . . was killed uselessly in the Great War" (*Servant of the Queen,* pp. 55–56). At the time they met in London Kathleen had occasion to reply to Yeats's remark as to how young she looked: "It's hard work being beautiful" (*Yeats, 1865–1939,* p. 164). The statement is amplified by Yeats in his poem written two or three years later. Margaret Rudd feels that the exchange in the poem "seems almost like a recorded conversation"—*Divided Image: A Study of William Blake and W. B. Yeats* (London, 1953), p. 148. But that factualness only attests to the more casual realism of the language the speaker has begun to use in the poetry of the middle period.

3. *On Poetry and Poets* (New York, 1961), p. 300. Eliot obviously takes exception to the view of Horatio Krans that "the idealism of the play is intangible and ineffective" (*Yeats and the Irish Literary Revival,* p. 132). Whether successful or

not as a play—see Leonard Nathan's analysis in *The Tragic Drama of William Butler Yeats: Figures in a Dance* (New York, 1965), pp. 72 ff.—it in any case constituted Yeats's "first attempt to dramatize 'the soul of man' "—Ann Saddlemyer, " 'The Heroic Discipline of the Looking-Glass': W. B. Yeats's Search for Dramatic Design," in *The World of W. B. Yeats: Essays in Perspective,* ed. Robin Skelton and Ann Saddlemyer (Victoria, 1965), p. 101. For this reason "the beauty of *The Shadowy Waters,*" as S. B. Bushrui points out, would tend to lie not in "character or action, but . . . speech and sentiment"—*Yeats's Verse-Plays: The Revisions, 1900–1910* (London, 1965), p. 38.

4. Richard Ellmann was the first to make this point—*Yeats: The Man and the Masks* (New York, 1948), p. 141.

5. *Yeats's Verse-Plays,* p. 1.

6. Bushrui noted that the early version, "about 1885, ended with Forgael leaving Dectora and setting out on his quest alone" (*ibid.,* p. 3). This is rather similar to Oisin's attitude to his solicitous companion, Niamh. Below, in the main text, I note also a similarity in the attitude of the speaker in "The Collar-Bone of a Hare."

7. Cf. *Man and the Masks,* p. 157.

8. *Identity of Yeats,* p. 81.

9. *Man and the Masks,* p. 125.

10. Disregard George Brandon Saul's suggestion that the poem has been misdated (*Prolegomena to Yeats's Poems,* p. 103). He refers to Hone's mistaken conjecture that Yeats was speaking of "The Collar-Bone of a Hare" in the letter to his father dated October 17, 1918—J. B. Yeats, *Letters to his Son W. B. Yeats and Others, 1869–1922,* ed. Joseph Hone (New York, 1946), p. 251. Yeats was quite obviously referring to the first of "Two Songs of a Fool" (*P,* 380).

11. As Marion Witt phrases it, "the spell dissolved in the poem is the spell of the world itself with its weary divisions and compromises. The poet sees through the symbol of death (or through death itself), and hence in perspective the 'old bitter world' "—"Yeats' 'The Collar-Bone of a Hare,' " *Explicator,* VII, iii (1948), item 21.

12. *Servant of the Queen,* p. 319.

13. Quoted in *Identity of Yeats,* p. 74.

14. *Man and the Masks,* pp. 220–21.

15. The poems, as they appear in *The Little Review*, IV, 9–12, follow roughly a reverse sequence, the most recent poem, "The Wild Swans at Coole," heading the group. "Broken Dreams" (Nov. 1915) rather than "The Collar-Bone of a Hare" (July 1915)—placed next to last—concludes the group of love poems, stressing the speaker's disillusionment with the past, as a kind of contrast to any transcending joy.

16. As John Unterecker claims, the identity of the three figures referred to is rather obvious: "the 'harlot' who had pretended to be with child in the hope of trapping Yeats into marriage, Iseult Gonne, and Maud herself"—*A Reader's Guide to William Butler Yeats* (New York, 1959), p. 143. But more is meant than just a biographical reference. The "child" is traditionally associated with "innocence"; in fin de siècle poetry the "harlot" has a ritual connotation. Compare what Jung says about the mystical conjunction of the three "types": the harlot "declares herself to be a conjunction of the sun and moon. . . . She is, in fact, mingled with the Beloved, from which it is evident that the perfect state melts *sponsus* [lover; spouse] and *sponsa* [beloved] into *one* figure, the sun-and-moon child"—*Mysterium Conjunctionis* (New York, 1963), pp. 443–44. Is this an explanation of Yeats's feeling that "Iseult has always been something like a daughter to me?" (*L*, 631).

17. Jeffares quite naturally associates the image of beauty with Iseult. *Yeats: Man and Poet*, pp. 190, 206.

18. *Ibid.*, p. 325, n. 65. S. B. Bushrui argues that "Yeats saw Solomon more through the *Arabian Nights* than the Old Testament" and that "Sheba too is not the Sheba of the Old Testament, but an Arab queen of dazzling beauty who was fit match for the great Solomon" ("Yeats's Arabic Interests," *In Excited Reverie*, pp. 309–10).

19. I am not as certain as is F. A. C. Wilson (*Yeats's Iconography*, pp. 279, 281 ff.) that Solomon and Sheba are to be seen as figures "nearly transfigured" by their love. Wilson regards the ventriloquism of the witch as a feature in the relationship that is to be taken "less than seriously."

20. William Wordsworth, *The Prelude*, II, l. 352.

21. Only by this circular route, through an expression of solitude, may it be said, to quote Graham Martin, that " 'The Gift of Harun Al-Rashid' finally overcomes the opposition between wisdom and love"—" 'The Wild Swans at Coole,' " in *An Honoured Guest*, ed. Denis Donoghue and J. R. Mulryne (New York, 1966), p. 64, *n.* 25.

22. For an amusing picture of the two—passing each other by, though looking for one another—see the cartoon used as a frontispiece in Oliver St. John Gogarty, *As I was Going Down Sackville St.* (New York, 1937). Yeats's head is tossed high. Russell's head is bent, as though eyeing the ground in profound reverie.

chapter 5

1. Jeffares, *Yeats, Man and Poet,* p. 141.

2. *Ibid.,* pp. 59–60.

3. Hone, *Yeats, 1865–1939,* p. 252.

4. Yeats first makes reference to the "phoenix" in his diary for January 1909. He is greatly agitated when he writes about the uncertain terms of his relationship with Maud Gonne. "Of old she was a phoenix and I feared her, but now she is my child more than my sweetheart. . . . Always since I was a boy I have questioned dreams for her sake—and she herself always a dream and deceiving hope . . . the phoenix nesting when she is reborn in all her power to torture and delight, to waste and to ennoble" (Moore, *The Unicorn,* pp. 202-203). In the poem he wrote in 1915 Yeats no longer suggests her cruelty or her transforming, redemptive power.

5. Thomas Whitaker traces her words to those of Coventry Patmore and Plutarch —*Swan and Shadow: Yeats's Dialogue with History* (Chapel Hill, 1964), pp. 159–60.

6. The poems suggest the process of enlightenment as undergone by a saint or Christ, contracting pain or stigmata ("riddled with light") as an antidote to pride and as a means of inducing a sense of charity, or love.

7. I would agree with Peter Ure in saying that the phrase "riddled with light" is "the highest point to which the poem mounts in its restless rush of movement and rising rhythms" (*Yeats,* p. 58). The word "riddled" suggests both the ecstatic— stigmatic—pain of physical transfiguration and the speaker's dumbfounded questioning of self-justifying motives, his faculties having momently been transfixed by the enigmatic disclosure of his own, absolute self-enlightenment.

8. T. R. Henn contends that "The Cold Heaven" "has the clarity and vehemence of a visionary moment: made credible and vivid by the epithet *rook-delighting.* The stark visual impression of the black rooks, in the wild acrobatics* [Henn's note: * Rooks and green plovers are among the few birds which seem to do this, in a kind of ecstasy] in which . . . they sometimes revel . . ." (" 'The Green Helmet' and 'Responsibilities,' " in *An Honoured Guest,* p. 51).

9. My reading of Yeats's word "responsibility" as deriving from the earlier connotation of "respond," "responsiveness," is not the reading applied by any critics, so far as I am aware, who have dealt with the volume *Responsibilities.* Stephen Spender's reading comes closest to my interpretation in that he relates the con-

ventional sense of the word to the poet's awareness of his inherent, imaginative response to reality: "What does Yeats . . . ultimately feel responsible towards? The answer is, perhaps, to an abstraction, to the imagination which creates. But nevertheless this abstraction is a quality within ourselves"—"The Influence of Yeats on Later English Poets," *Tri-Quarterly*, IV (1965), 89. Compare also Priscilla Shaw's statement: Yeats was "both moral and responsible, and the surface irresponsibility or 'aestheticism' of some of his poems is clearly a reaction to the impossibility of adequate moral action, rather than some unthinking impulse" (*Rilke, Valéry and Yeats*, pp. 218–19).

10. The proleptic intent of the poem, to paraphrase a remark of Hart Crane's, is best construed with regard to poetic or psychopoetic, not historical, necessity— "Modern Poetry," in *Collected Poems of Hart Crane*, ed. Waldo Frank (Garden City, 1958), p. 182. Compare Thomas Parkinson's remark about one of the five possible "modes" in which the narrator in Yeats's poems speaks: "poems of pure revelation— what Yeats himself would have considered pure poetry—are possible only within the impure content of the life of the divided self struggling through successive nightmares of deceptive lures"—*W. B. Yeats: The Later Poetry* (Berkeley, 1964), p. 54. Is it necessary to conclude, therefore, as does R. P. Blackmur (among others) that the "magic" of revelation in "The Second Coming" "promises . . . exact prediction of events in the natural world" ("The Later Poetry of W. B. Yeats," in *Permanence of Yeats*, p. 49)?

11. Johannes Kleinstück has dealt in greatest depth with the psychological implications of the poem: ". . . *der Bezugspunkt, um es so zu sagen, war der Mensch in seiner Gottebenbildlichkeit; das Unmenschliche am Menschen war zwar nicht ohne Wirkung und Wirklichkeit, aber man erkannte es nicht als Ideal an. Jetzt ist es, als ob sich das Unmenschliche für diese Nicht-Anerkennung rächen wollte; was unterdrückt war, kommt nach oben.*" ["The point of relation, as it were, has to do with man in his likeness to God; the unhuman man was not indeed without consequence or reality, but it was not recognized as an ideal. Now it is as if for this lack of recognition the unhuman would take revenge; what was repressed comes to the surface."] Suppression of brutish qualities, Kleinstück implies, before the elevated ideal of God, is symbolized in Western consciousness by obeisance of the three kings from the East (*"grausamsten Tyrannen"*) before Jesus; and the reverse movement would be symbolized quite naturally by the figure of a beast slouching, ready to spring—"W. B. Yeats: *The Second Coming*. Eine Studie zur Interpretation und Kritik," *Die Neuren Sprachen* (July, 1961), 306. John Unterecker also takes cognizance of the unconscious tendency in men to make their own mortality reason for wishing upon the world universal destruction (*A Reader's Guide to Yeats*, pp. 164–65).

12. Cleanth Brooks makes the puzzling statement that the poem is seen in the context of "Phase 23"—offering no substantial argument for his proposition ("Yeats: The Poet as Mythmaker," in *Permanence of Yeats*, p. 72). T. R. Henn, regarding what the poem describes rather than the state of mind of the narrator, assigns

"The Second Coming" to the "primary" phases 2 to 7, *The Lonely Tower: Studies in the Poetry of W. B. Yeats* (London, 1949), p. 190.

chapter 6

1. *Last Romantics*, p. 233.

2. The terms are interrelated as Yeats used them in *A Vision*. In moving from an integrated awareness of self toward total social awareness one begins regarding oneself as an object more and more at one with other "objects" in the world around him—leading to a feeling of transpersonal kinship by which all things seem linked, joined in a "unity of being." Ultimate "unity of being," Yeats recognized (in *The Autobiography*), was impossible to realize except in the form of a vision. For clarification of this point see Northrop Frye," The Rising of the Moon: A Study of 'A Vision,' " in *An Honoured Guest*, pp. 16–17.

3. Quoted in Ellmann, *Identity of Yeats*, p. 245.

4. Hone, *Yeats: 1865–1939*, p. 325.

5. *A Vision*, pp. 214–15.

6. Quoted in *Yeats: 1865–1939*, p. 244.

7. The quote concludes: "The last kiss is given to the void." This suggests the mystic's *nada*, and we can be sure Yeats had in mind the Hindu or Buddhist psycho-eschatology. But Yeats always draws back from the Eastern extreme. Compare this note of his made for the second edition of *A Vision:* "If consciousness is indeed conflict must not the phaseless sphere ["Phase 1"] from which all comes and to which all returns and source of all value be unconscious, and annihilation, as some say the early Buddhists thought, end all our effort? I have come to see, however, that their conflict resolves itself into the antinomies of Kant and that we must say of the ultimate reality as the early Buddhists themselves said, 'We do not know that it exists, we do not know that it does not exist,' and as the early Buddhists did not, that we can express it by a series of contradictions" (quoted in *Identity of Yeats*, pp. 234–35).

8. *Swan and Shadow*, pp. 171 ff.

9. *Inferno,* trans. Dorothy Sayers (New York, 1963) Canto XXXIII, l. 58.

10. In a note appended to all but the first two printings of the poem, Yeats refers disparagingly to the hawk as perhaps symbolizing "the straight road of logic, and so of mechanism" (*P*, 827). The hawk is the "gloomy bird of prey" that belies true wisdom, referred to by Tom O'Roughley (*P*, 338). Compare also the poem

entitled "The Hawk" (*P,* 349): "What tumbling cloud did you cleave, / Yellow-eyed hawk of the mind, / . . . that I . . . / . . . / Should give to my friend / A pretence of wit.' "

11. Cf. Frye, "The Rising of the Moon," in *An Honoured Guest,* pp. 16–17.

12. For the most extensive account to date of Chatterjee's influence on Yeats, see F. F. Farag, "Oriental and Celtic Elements in the Poetry of W. B. Yeats," *Yeats, 1865–1965: Essays,* pp. 33–51.

13. Is this what Conor Cruise O'Brien has in mind when he discusses such poems as "Leda" and "The Second Coming" and considers the "connection . . . between the politics and the poetry" of Yeats? "There is a deeper connection" between the two, O'Brien declares, "if the political prose and the poetry are thought of as . . . cognate expressions of a fundamental force, anterior to both politics and poetry" ("Passion and Cunning," *In Excited Reverie,* p. 274).

14. " 'Leda and the Swan,' " *The Times* (London) *Literary Supplement,* July 2, 1962, p. 532. Madge himself had advanced the proposition that the relief of Leda and the swan in the British Museum provided the source for Yeats's "Leda." Giorgio Melchiori has enthusiastically acceded to Madge's argument, noting that earlier drafts of the poem match closely the depiction on the Museum relief (*The Times* (London) *Literary Supplement,* August 3, 1962, p. 557). K. G. Cross, with uncharacteristic precipitance, follows the suggestion of Madge and Melchiori and claims the relief "exactly fits the description of the rape of Leda in Yeats's poem" ("The Fascination of What's Difficult: A Survey of Yeats Criticism and Research," *In Excited Reverie,* p. 53). Charles Gullans, though perhaps overemphatic in his argument, challenges the notion that excludes all but one source for Yeats's poem. "In the woodcut," Gullans claims, "[Leda] is both 'staggering' and 'terrified,' but in the relief, far from being terrified or off-balance, she seems actually to be assisting at her own seduction." Arguing against the claim Melchiori made in his *Whole Mystery of Art* and in the *Times* article, "regarding the priority of visual over intellectual stimuli for Yeats" (Melchiori, *The Times,* August 3) Gullans maintains that "however close the pictorial details . . . Yeats could well have composed his sonnet without any particular pictorial referent in mind." He then proposes that Yeats may well have written his poem as a direct reply to the less tightly knit ode of Moore, "the only literary source that I know for any one of the most impressive passages in the [Yeats] sonnet." The argument need not stop with Gullans' final concession that all three—the relief, the woodcut, the ode—"explain every feature of all the versions of 'Leda and the Swan' " (*The Times Literary Supplement,* November 9, 1962, p. 864). Obviously the accreditation of sources depends upon their interpretation and the interpretation of the work presumably based on them. I prefer to hold up the poem as its own example, and by suggesting the richness of its ambiguity open the door against specific sources. For a similar attitude to "sources" see Ellmann, *Identity of Yeats,* (2nd ed.; New York, 1964), pp. vii–viii.

15. My appraisal differs from Ellmann's latest view of the poem, that "we watch Leda's reaction, not the god's" (*Identity of Yeats,* 2nd ed., p. viii).

16. The most convincing discussion of this point is to be found in Shaw's *Rilke, Valéry and Yeats,* pp. 180–81.

17. "The Later Poetry of W. B. Yeats," in *Permanence of Yeats,* p. 58. Edward Engelberg follows Blackmur in proposing a unifying consciousness, behind the poem, for associations resulting in or suggested by the poem (*The Vast Design,* p. 115). John F. Adams regards the duality in the poem as a form of psychological projection (in this respect my own analysis approximates that of Adams): "With the wings beating 'above the staggering girl,' Leda, it is insisted, is a woman, 'staggering' beneath the dual reality of the swan as swan and the oppressive dream figure from the unconscious, or the psychological reality behind the physical, sexual reality"—" 'Leda and the Swan': The Aesthetics of Rape," *Bucknell Review,* XII, xiii (1964), 51.

18. "On Yeats's Poem 'Leda and the Swan,'" *Modern Philology,* LI (1954), 271.

19. " 'Leda and the Swan,' " p. 51.

20. *The Oxford Universal Dictionary on Historical Principles* (Oxford, 1965), p. 2155.

21. Adams sees the anticipation of sexual climax described in the ambiguous image in line 7, "that white rush": "The seminal implications are obvious; its violence suggests both the god-like ejaculation and the overpoweringness of both on the imprisoned female" (" 'Leda and the Swan,' " p. 54).

22. I believe Richard Ellmann mistakes the terms of the poem by supposing that it is sexual passion and not lack of unitive knowledge, or understanding, which Yeats regards as the ultimately destructive agent in history (*Identity of Yeats,* 2nd ed., p. viii).

23. *Whole Mystery of Art,* p. 91.

24. Quoted in *Identity of Yeats,* p. 147.

25. *The Unicorn,* p. 242.

26. *Ibid.,* p. 146.

27. *Lonely Tower,* p. 125.

28. Cf. Israel Regardie, *The Golden Dawn* (Chicago, 1937–1940), IV, p. 214: "The tremendous destructive influence of the lightning, rendering asunder established

forms to make way for new forms to emerge, revolution as distinguished from transmutation or sublimity, the destructive as opposed to the conservative, energy attacking inertia, the impetuous ejection of those who would enclose themselves in the walls of ease and tradition."

29. Sarah Youngblood makes the interesting observation that unlike the poem *Meditations in Time of Civil War* in which the image of the tower "is everywhere evident as image and setting," in "The Tower" the tower as symbol "is everywhere assured and seldom evident"; and "that the tower as a phallic symbol, insofar as it becomes subtly identified with the condition of the poet himself, is a phallic symbol *manqué*. This may explain the small part it plays explicitly in the poem."—"A Reading of *The Tower*," *Twentieth Century Literature*, V (1959), 79.

30. Youngblood regards the "unseeing / Plunge" as "a metaphor for the sexual act, as a metaphor also for the plunge into experience which is reality." (*Ibid.*, p. 80).

31. *Whole Mystery of Art*, pp. 126–27.

32. Yeats must have found a curious satisfaction in continually calling the local builder who renovated the tower, Thomas Rafferty, by the name of the luckless bard Raftery (*L*, 628 ff.).

33. *Yeats, Man and Poet*, p. 216.

34. Quoted in *The Unicorn*, p. 202.

35. Quoted in *Yeats, Man and Poet*, p. 141.

36. *The Unicorn*, p. 38.

37. *Ibid.*, p. 197. Unless otherwise specified, information about the spiritual marriage is taken from Miss Moore's transcription and résumé of the journals, pp. 197–207 in *The Unicorn*. For the last four years of her life Mrs. Yeats had been generally adamant in refusing permission to consult the private journals of Yeats that were in her possession.

38. The dream process suggests an antithetical pull between spiritual and physical forces, the annunciation heralded by dove and archangel, and an unconscious suppression of physical-sexual violence. The account agrees with John F. Adams' thesis as to the nature of "Leda and the Swan": "the poem presents a sexual nightmare, the troubled expression of the unconscious in terms of a dream experience, and relates this dream experience to waking reality" (" 'Leda and the Swan,' " p. 49).

39. In light of this experience it is clear why he should follow his father's advice— or Blake's—in making the expression of passionate energy the primary concern of

the spiritual imagination, for "what is passion but the straining of man's being against some obstacle that obstructs its unity" (*Ex,* 252).

chapter 7

1. Donald Torchiana has researched the original circumstances leading to the writing of this poem. He notes that the children in the school Yeats had seen were being brought up under the Montessori method. Though Yeats would heartily agree with the ends of the Montessori method as described by Giovanni Gentile, and as reported by Torchiana, it is doubtful whether he so heartily approves of the situation he describes in "Among School Children" ("'Among School Children': the Irish Spirit," *In Excited Reverie,* pp. 123–50). On the other hand the speaker in the poem does not regard the schoolroom situation so wryly as does John Wain— "W. B. Yeats: 'Among School Children,'" *Interpretations: Essays on Twelve English Poems,* ed. John Wain (London, 1955), pp. 203–204. My own tendency is to regard the schoolroom situation as a half-way house, fit material for the poetic proposition evolved in the last stanza of the poem.

2. For discussion of the term "self-born" see Patricia Terwilliger, "A Re-interpretation of Stanzas VII and VIII of W. B. Yeats's *Among School Children,*" *Boston University Studies in English,* V (1961), p. 32.

3. "Dance and the Soul," *Dialogues* (New York, 1956), p. 55.

4. *Romantic Image* (London, 1957), p. 60.

5. *The Well-Wrought Urn* (New York, 1947), p. 187.

6. The crux of the poem concerns the nature of the "harmony" and "unity" of the images and point of view in the last stanza. Patricia Terwilliger argues for both the unity and harmony of the last stanza: "It is as if the poet were asking how anyone could remain unconvinced of the oneness of reality if he were confronted with the spontaneously beautiful chestnut tree and the dancer [i.e., images of "natural spontaneous beauty"], and it is precisely because Yeats does confront the reader directly with these images of the unity of beauty that the reader as well as the poet not only recognizes but participates in the triumphant affirmation," "A Re-interpretation of Stanzas VII and VIII of W. B. Yeats's *Among School Children,*" pp. 33–34. Margaret Rudd emphasizes more the point of view of the speaker: In the next to last stanza Yeats "is talking about the unbridgeable gap between appearance and reality, body and spirit. And he asks in the last stanza why this should be, since in all fine and lovely things spirit and matter seem indivisible" *Divided Image,* p. 177. Edmund Wilson ("W. B. Yeats," in *Permanence of Yeats,* p. 37) and Northrop Frye ("The Rising of the Moon," in *An Honoured Guest,* p. 28) both regard the culminating lines holding in unity and yet in contrast the several images and feelings described therein. Brooks, on the other hand, sees an ontological irony in the speaker's attempt to realize or

"possess" what he sees and expresses (*The Well-Wrought Urn,* p. 190). My own view most nearly approximates that of Brooks and Thomas Parkinson. The latter regards the poem as being "in part pre-poetic" and "concerned with the conditions of poetic apprehension." "The poem [in the last stanza] flirts with the danger of casting doubt on its own resolutions, largely because it exhibits in its dramaturgy a multiple poetics" *Yeats, The Later Poetry,* pp. 51–52.

7. "Yeats's 'Byzantium,' "*Critical Quarterly,* II (1960), p. 252. For exposition of a view contrary to Fraser's view of the poem as representation of the artistic process see Frederick Grubb, *A Vision of Reality: A Study of Liberalism in Twentieth-Century Verse* (London, 1965), p. 34 and A. N. Jeffares, "Yeats's Byzantine Poems and the Critics," *English Studies in Africa,* V (1962), 23. Jeffares' essay is important for summarizing the research and criticism done until 1961 on the Byzantium poems. Criticism of the poem is most radically divided over how Yeats cast his lot, for the fixed ideal or for the flux of life—see, for example, Shaw, *Rilke, Valéry and Yeats,* p. 204; F. A. C. Wilson, *W. B. Yeats and Tradition* (London, 1958), pp. 231 ff. And David Daiches, *Poetry and the Modern World* (Chicago, 1940), p. 184; B. L. Reid, *William Butler Yeats: The Lyric of Tragedy* (Norman, 1961), p. 201; Grubb, *Vision of Reality,* p. 34.

8. Moore, *The Unicorn,* p. 217.

9. Peter Ure assumes that Yeats's description of the somnambulist is part of that passage "which is an exact enough description of these poems [the two Byzantium poems]"—*Towards a Mythology* (London, 1946), p. 68. Ure, however, does not pursue the matter further. Fraser, speaking of "the Byzantium of the poem" feels that "we explore it like a city in a dream" ("Yeats's 'Byzantium,' " p. 256).

10. "Yeats: The Poet as Myth-Maker," in *Permanence of Yeats,* pp. 77 ff.

11. Cf. Melchiori, *The Whole Mystery of Art,* pp. 206, 224 ff.

12. T. R. Henn feels that "the flood symbolizes the irrational, the confusion, the pattern . . ." which is put in order by "the formal ceremonious art of Byzantium" (*Lonely Tower,* p. 222). An early draft of the poem indicates that at one time at least Yeats wanted to make reference to breaking "the bleak glittering intricacies [*sic*] aimless flood of imagery"—Jon Stallworthy, *Between the Lines* (Oxford, 1963), p. 129.

13. *Identity of Yeats,* 2nd ed., p. 221. Both William Empson—"Mr. Wilson on the Byzantine Poems," *Review of English Literature,* I (1960), 55—and Anne Kostelanetz—"Irony in Yeats's Byzantine Poems," *Tennessee Studies in Literature,* IX (1964), 137—have also regarded the bird as an ironic product of its self-demeaning scorn.

14. For a summary of the controversy over Yeats's use of the two words, "disdain" and "distain" see Melchiori, *Whole Mystery of Art,* pp. 207–208.

15. Unterecker was the first to draw attention to the significance of the repetition in "Byzantium" (*A Reader's Guide to Yeats*, pp. 219–20). Of the other poems of Yeats, only "The Cap and Bells" compares with "Byzantium" in incidence of verbal repetition.

16. Worth noting in this regard is the suggestion of Balachandra Rajan that Yeats's notion of tragic joy has significant implications for drama of the absurd: "the great strength of [Yeats's] strategy (for those few who have the creative power to employ it) is that the absurd is virtually turned upon itself; it becomes merely the ultimate provocation by which man's dignity is established and intensified. Tragic joy, the heroic cry in the midst of despair," is a "differing [i.e., different] formulation of this basic response"—"Yeats and the Absurd," *Tri-Quarterly*, IV (1965), 131.

17. *Plays for an Irish Theatre* (London, 1911), pp. ix–x.

18. "Yeats and Fascism: What Rough Beast," *New Statesman*, February 26, 1965, pp. 319–22.

19. That is, in the last volume published in his own lifetime, *New Poems* (Dublin, 1938). For the controversy over the order of poems in Yeats's so-called "Last Poems" see Curtis Bradford, "Yeats's 'Last Poems' Again," No. VIII of *The Dolmen Press Yeats Centenary Papers* (Dublin, 1965), pp. 263 ff.

20. Identification of the reference is far from certain. My own identification coincides with that of Vivienne Koch, who first correlated "Rocky Face" with the antithetical self—*W. B. Yeats: The Tragic Phase* (London, 1951), pp. 99–100. See also Reid, *Lyric of Tragedy*, p. 212, J. R. Mulryne ("The 'Last Poems,'" in *An Honoured Guest*, pp. 125–26), and Curtis Bradford, *Yeats at Work* (Carbondale, 1965), p. 148 ("in Mrs. Yeats's annotated copy of *Last Poems* Rocky Face is glossed as 'Delphic Oracle' ").

21. Any defense of the unity of the poem would have to depend upon justification of the radical shift from images of flux to the final image of artistic stasis. Thomas Whitaker offers the most convincing argument in this respect, though he does not attempt to demonstrate any real meeting point for separated images and points of view in the poem (*Swan and Shadow*, pp. 277–78). A. N. Jeffares recognizes the problem of the disjuncture in the poem, but supposes that Yeats's letter to Dorothy Wellesley (that "the east has its solutions always and therefore knows nothing of tragedy"—*LP*, 8–9) satisfies the requirement of the poem as poem—"Notes on Yeats's 'Lapis Lazuli,'" *Modern Language Notes*, LXV (1950), 491. Richard Ellmann and John Unterecker both follow Jeffares' leads in using the letter to justify the compositional effect of the poem.

22. Vivienne Koch makes the appealing suggestion that "the 'fat Dreamer' is stressed in such a way that, for the moment, he *becomes* Buddha" (*The Tragic*

Phase, p. 72). However regarded, the direction of movement in the poem is forward and backward in time, evolving *toward* an imageless and timeless—Buddha-like—awareness. Cf. Unterecker, *A Reader's Guide to Yeats,* p. 281, and Whitaker, *Swan And Shadow,* pp. 240–41.

23. One is reminded of the use to which the sculpted image as antiself is put in "Ego Dominus Tuus," "The Gyres," "The Second Coming," "Lapis Lazuli," "A Bronze Head." " 'Body,' " says J. R. Mulryne, "by espousal of the sculpted image becomes 'soul' " ("The 'Last Poems,' " in *An Honoured Guest,* p. 129).

24. Lines 44–46 of the "Ninth Elegy," *Duino Elegies,* trans. Stephen Spender and J. B. Leishman (New York, 1963; original edition, 1938), p. 75.

25. *The Lyric of Tragedy,* p. 240. For an opposite point of view see J. R. Mulryne, "The 'Last Poems,' " in *An Honoured Guest,* p. 140. Mulryne parallels, rather than contrasts "High Talk" with "The Circus Animals' Desertion," and therefore regards the former as an "ironic valuation," a poem in which we are made to pity, or laugh at, Malachi, rather than to admire his achievement. I suggest that it would have been untypical of Yeats to deliberately underlay with irony the sustained buoyancy, or the nonchalance, that went into the making of a poem such as "High Talk."

26. Quoted in David R. Clark, " 'Metaphors for Poetry': W. B. Yeats and the Occult," *The World of W. B. Yeats,* p. 54.

27. Curtis Bradford claims that "High Talk" was begun July 29, 1938, and that "The Circus Animals' Desertion" was written between November 1937 and September 1938 ("Yeats 'Last Poems' Again," p. 286).

index

Bernard Levine is assistant professor of English at Wayne State University. He received the A.B. degree (1956) from Harvard University and the Ph.D. degree (1965) from Brown University. He has written several journal articles on the works of W. B. Yeats.

The manuscript was edited by Linda Grant. The book was designed by Mary Jowski. The typefaces used are Linotype Granjon recut under the supervision of George W. Jones and based on a face originally designed by Claude Garamond. The display face is also Granjon.

The book is printed on Warren's Olde Style Antique and bound in Bancroft's Linen Finished Cloth over boards. Manufactured in the United States of America.